ETHICS AND THE PROFESSIONS

Ethics and the Professions

Edited by
RUTH F. CHADWICK

Avebury

Aldershot · Brookfield USA · Hong Kong · Singapore · Sydney

Published by
Avebury
Ashgate Publishing Limited
Gower House
Croft Road
Aldershot
Hants GU11 3HR
England

Ashgate Publishing Company
Old Post Road
Brookfield
Vermont 05036
USA

British Library Cataloguing in Publication Data

Ethics and the Professions. – (Avebury
Series in Philosophy)
  I. Chadwick, Ruth F. II. Series
  174

  ISBN 1-85628-632-0

Library of Congress Cataloging-in-Publication Data

Ethics and the professions / [edited by] Ruth Chadwick.
      p.   cm. -- (Avebury series in philosophy)
    Papers based on the 1993 annual conference of the Society for
Applied Philosophy. Holly Royde House, Manchester.
      ISBN 1-85628-632-0 : £32.50 ($59.950 (U.S.) approx.)
      1. Professional ethics--Great Britain--Congresses.
    2. Responsibility--Congresses. I. Chadwick, Ruth F.   II. Series.
BJ1725.E88 1994
174--dc20   94-32825
                                                                    CIP

Typeset by
Jane Erskine

Printed in Great Britain by Ipswich Book Co. Ltd., Ipswich,
Suffolk

Contents

List of contributors

Timo Airaksinen is Professor of Philosophy (Ethics and Social Philosophy) at the University of Helsinki. He has published extensively on history of philosophy (Hegel, Berkeley and Hobbes), epistemology (foundationalism vs. coherentism) and ethics, especially applied ethics. He is the head of department and assistant dean of the Faculty of Social Sciences. Some of his books are *Ethics of Coercion and Authority* (Pittsburgh University Press, 1988) and *Of Glamor, Sex and de Sade* (Longwood Academic, 1991). He is currently working on Hobbes and the emotions, and professional ethics.

Ruth Chadwick is Professor of Moral Philosophy at the Centre for Professional Ethics, University of Central Lancashire. Her publications include *Ethics Reproduction and Genetic Control* (Routledge, 1992). With Andrew Belsey she edited *Ethical Issues in Journalism and the Media* (Routledge, 1992). They are also joint editors of the Routledge series on Professional Ethics.

Andrew Edgar is a lecturer in Philosophy and Acting Director of the Centre for Applied Ethics, University of Wales, College of Cardiff. The author of several articles on applied ethics and critical theory, he is currently co-ordinating a European Union funded concerted action on the ethics of health care allocation.

Bill Fulford is a Research Fellow at Green College in Oxford and an Honorary Consultant Psychiatrist. He is the founder of the Philosophy Group in the Royal College of Psychiatrists and Editor of a new Journal, *PPP - Philosophy, Psychiatry and Psychology*. He is the Director of the Oxford Practice Skills Programme, an experimental course for medical students in ethics, law and communication skills. He has published widely on the ethics and philosophy of psychiatry and medicine, and is the author of *Moral Theory and Medical Practice* (Cambridge University Press, 1990).

Nigel Harris is a senior lecturer in Philosophy at the University of Dundee. He is the author of *Professional Codes of Conduct in the United Kingdom: A Directory* (Mansell, London, 1989) and has published articles on ethical issues that arise in various particular professions including accountancy, social work, journalism and medicine.

Heta Häyry is Docent and Assistant Professor of Practical Philosophy at the University of Helsinki and Docent of the Philosophy of Law at the University of Lapland. She is an adviser to the Finnish National Board of Health and Social Security on social ethics and health care ethics, and a member of the Research Council for the Humanities in the Academy of Finland. Her publications in English include *The Limits of Medical Paternalism* (Routledge, 1991) and many articles on health care ethics and general philosophy.

Matti Häyry is Docent and Junior Research Fellow in Practical Philosophy at the University of Helsinki and Docent of Bioethics at the University of Tampere. He is an adviser to the Finnish National Board of Health and Social Security on bioethics. His publications in English include *Liberal Utilitarianism and Applied Ethics* (Routledge, 1994) and many articles on bioethics and general philosophy in academic journals.

Christine Henry is Professor of Applied Ethics and Head of the Centre for Professional Ethics at the University of Central Lancashire. She was project leader for Ethics and Values Audit. Her published works include three books co-authored with G. Pashley on *Health Care Research, Health Ethics and Health Psychology* (Quay Publishing, 1990-91). She jointly edited a scholarly reader entitled *Themes and Perspectives in Nursing* with K. Soothill and K. Kendrick (Chapman and Hall, 1992).

Dick Holdsworth is Head of the STOA Team (Scientific and Technological Options Assessment Programme), Directorate-General for Research, European Parliament, Luxembourg.

Jennifer Jackson is Director of the Centre for Business and Professional Ethics and Senior Lecturer in the Department of Philosophy at the University of Leeds. She has published a number of articles in the field of applied ethics.

Jenneth Parker is a part-time tutor at CCE, University of Sussex, consultant for Education for sustainability, and is currently researching for a DPhil in Ecofeminist Ethics in the Womens' Studies Graduate Division, Sussex.

Win Tadd is a Senior Nurse Tutor at the South East Wales Institute of Nursing and Midwifery Education in Cardiff. She co-authored, with Ruth Chadwick, *Ethics and Nursing Practice* (Macmillan, 1992)

Richard Tur is Benn Law Fellow at Oriel College, Oxford and Visiting Fellow at the National Institute for Law, Ethics and Public Affairs, Faculty of Law, Griffith University, Brisbane, Australia.

Preface

Ruth Chadwick

The papers in this volume are based on the 1993 annual conference of the Society for Applied Philosophy, held at Holly Royde House, Manchester on the theme of Ethics and the Professions.

Professional Ethics is now a subject of considerable debate for several reasons. The first concerns changes in society: long established professions have had to face challenges to their traditional power and authority, both from increasingly knowledgeable and vocal client and consumer groups and from government. In medicine, for example, the growth of importance of autonomy has undermined the tradition of paternalism and with it the godlike status of the doctor. Changes in the National Health Service have exalted skills of management rather than medical expertise. On the other hand more and more groups have been aspiring to professional status. The change in the image of nursing is a case in point here, marked by the move from the view that the role of the nurse was to be loyal to the doctor, to the ideal of the nurse as an accountable practitioner.

Developments in applied ethics have also contributed to the growth in the discussion of professional ethics. These include debates at the theoretical level both as to what it means to apply ethics to a particular field of activity, and as to what philosophical tradition is appropriately applied. Then there is the elucidation of the philosophical and ethical problems raised by the particular subject area itself. It is fair to say that the marked expansion in applied ethics in the last three decades has to a considerable extent arisen from the interchange between ethics and medicine. This has now given rise to similar work in relation to other professional or quasi-professional groups.

So what is a profession? This is the first question this collection of essays sets out to address. There are three explicit themes in the volume, each of which could be seen as a contribution to it. The first theme examines the nature of professions; the second the importance of accountability as a defining characteristic of the professional; the third the nature and significance of professional codes, which are sometimes seen as a sine qua non of a professional group. The role of ethical theory is taken up in several papers: Nigel Harris, for example, looks at the relationship between Kantian ethics and codes of conduct; Andrew Edgar contrasts a principlist approach with narrative ethics, drawing on the work of Paul Ricoeur; Richard Tur discusses role ethics and virtue ethics in the course of his analysis of accountability and lawyers.

The papers dealing explicitly with the first theme (although the division is to a certain extent artificial) are those of Timo Airaksinen, Bill Fulford and Jenneth Parker. Timo Airaksinen looks at the importance of an ideal of service and a body of scientific knowledge in professional life and his analysis leads him to draw a contrast between what he regards as a genuine profession, such as medicine, and a pseudo-profession such as engineering. He argues that unlike medicine, which works to promote health, engineers do not have any key values that are internal to their practice.

Bill Fulford makes the point that the training a professional group receives to a large extent determines its identity, and it is therefore important to examine this. Using the specific example of medicine, he argues that the traditional emphasis on the scientific model needs to be balanced by an input of a different kind. Fulford suggests that 'practice skills', including ethics and communication skills, are perhaps the essence of a professional.

Jenneth Parker turns the spotlight on moral philosophers themselves. Taking as her starting point Illich's criticism of the professions as disabling she asks whether philosophy is a profession and whether moral philosophers might be disabling rather than enabling in their role on expert committees. She argues that philosophy is a profession, but points to two senses of moral expertise. The moral philosopher's expertise lies not in having privileged access to moral truth but in enabling debate.

Accountability is taken up in the essays of Dick Holdsworth, Richard Tur and Win Tadd. Dick Holdsworth takes a professional to be a knowledge based worker in a defined domain, and his discussion explores accountability in technology assessment. Since knowledge is not equally shared, those who have it must give an account of themselves. Accountability, however, is not limited to giving an account when things have gone wrong. Holdsworth argues for a concept of accountability that is ongoing and dynamic. The professions exist within a society viewed as a community of knowledge in which there is a mutual obligation to provide accounts.

Richard Tur takes on board accountability in the legal profession.

Exploring the dilemmas posed for the lawyer in the adversarial system, with its duty of confidentiality to and support for the individual client, Tur argues that while the prevailing model of lawyers' ethics is instrumentalist, there is room for an alternative account in terms of virtue. Virtuous lawyers should be judged not by results but by judgement and their adherence to values internal to law. They are required to achieve a balance between conflicting objectives, of which accountability and independence are two.

Win Tadd explores the notion of accountability in relation to the nurse. The UKCC, the statutory body for nursing, has placed considerable emphasis on the idea that nurses are individually accountable for their actions. Tadd questions whether this is adequate in the absence of a critical examination of the other factors that impinge on the nurse's room for action, such as the environment of care and the managerial structure. Without this, the insistence on accountability can be seen as another problem for the nurse, rather than empowering.

The third and final theme of the volume is codes of professional conduct. Nigel Harris explores the extent to which they are based on ethical theory. An analysis of the form of clauses in codes suggests that they are Kantian in nature, but closer inspection reveals certain characteristics that are difficult to reconcile with Kantian ethics. The very fact that a code emanates from a source external to the professional is problematic. Harris suggests, however, that we should not conclude that codes are not Kantian, or worse, that they have no moral basis at all, but that as Kantian principles they are flawed. This gives a starting point for thinking about how to improve them.

Jennifer Jackson tackles the vexed question of the usefulness of codes, in the light of the often voiced criticism that they are open to varying interpretation. Jackson draws a distinction between variation in application, which is inevitable and acceptable, and variation in interpretation, which is potentially damaging. She calls for constructive dialogue to facilitate a shared understanding of what a code means.

Andrew Edgar explores the notion of codes of professional conduct as providers of narrative accounts which professionals can use to explain their actions. Narratives typically have characters and he uses a comparative analysis of the British and American social work codes to elucidate the different images of the professional provided by the two codes. The British code, for example, allows that the professional is vulnerable to failure.

Heta and Matti Häyry argue that the existence of a profession is based on human needs and values. Professionals sometimes have to perform actions which by any other standards would be unjustifiable, because they cause harm. The harm is counterbalanced by the satisfaction of the needs that the profession exists to satisfy. A code serves the function of justifying such actions and thus acts as a protective shield which explicates the rights and duties that professionals have. This analysis helps us to see the limitations of the claims of certain groups to professional status and privileges, if they are not satisfying a basic human need, and suggests a criterion to use in times of change, both in relation to human needs and to the claims of professional groups.

The final essay, by Christine Henry, looks at professional ethics in practice, asking if professionals practise what they preach. She argues, however, that much depends on the organizational structures within which they operate, and draws on an Ethics and Values Audit carried out at the University of Central Lancashire to illustrate the need for organizations to provide the environment in which professionals can live up to codes and mission statements.

I should like to thank all the contributors to this volume, the Society for Applied Philosophy for agreeing to a conference on this topic, especially Brenda Almond and the other members of the Executive Committee at the time. Thanks are also due to Avebury, for their patience in awaiting the copy. Most of all, I owe a great deal to Jeanne Verhagen and Jane Erskine for their assistance and support in producing the text.

Ruth Chadwick
University of Central Lancashire
Preston, UK.
1994

1 Service and science in professional life

Timo Airaksinen

I

From a sociological point of view, professions are characterized by their members' personal scientific competence and collective service ideal.[1] Thus professionals are benevolent experts who can justify their claims to authority and social power on this very basis. Their work has a solid foundation and as such their social mode of being conforms to the ideas of enlightenment. The story of a profession refers both to its ideals which are seen as undeniably good, and its science, which is seen as valid. Outside the professions we find a number of competitors, labelled as charlatans and impostors. Actually anyone who is left outside receives such a negative characterization.

Such a sociological picture looks interesting, especially as it involves values and ideals. At the same time, as we know, sociology as an empirical social science is not well equipped to handle these normative problems.[2] Such a shortcoming can be avoided by saying that all we need to study are social beliefs about values, and not the values themselves. In this manner values are reduced to social facts, or what people say about values. Professional values are what people happen to think of their work and its goals. Because values are difficult, a sociologist tends to emphasize science and professional education.

This methodological strategy tends to leave out something important, namely, such traditional professions as medicine, education, law, and social work deal with values which come as close to being objective values as possible. Health, learning, justice and welfare are value notions in such a strong sense that the denial of their validity is incomprehensible. In other words, if people do not appreciate health, they are somehow wrong. They should appreciate it, and they would, were their attitudes correct.

1

The same can be said of justice and welfare. It is of course a difficult question as to what the exact content of these notions is and how it is produced.

Values allow us to define service ideals. They allow us also to criticize professions and even assume a cynical view of professional life. Perhaps professions use ideal descriptions of their work only as a protective shield which conceals their real concerns. Money and power are the obvious motivational alternatives. Medicine becomes more and more like any other private business in a market where one can buy anything, if one can afford it. And what you buy from the medical market need not have any intimate connection to health, in the narrow and traditional sense of the term. Lawyers may not care about justice or even legality in a strict sense, but they aim at sharing the power and privileges of their employers. Whether the cynical view is valid or not, professions must be criticized.[3]

Professional science can also be criticized. Medicine may be a strong science, in the sense that its theories are first verified and then successfully applied to reality. But what about psychiatry? Is Freudian psychoanalysis the kind of science whose use to patients is justifiable?[4] Is education based on the scientific study of learning, or is education still a field of traditional work? What about the social care of alcoholics? What is the role of science here?

It seems that many traditional professions combine strong values and a dubious scientific expertise, a concealed fact possibly dismissed in sociology. Medicine looks first like an exception, but when one discusses nursing science and psychiatry one must be content to say that there are aspects even of medicine that are definitely problematic. Nevertheless, modern medicine is and remains the paradigmatic profession. All other professions live according to its model in order to acquire similar authority and power.

II

Such reflections are based on social science. Certainly professions inspire philosophical thoughts as well. These are often taken to fall under the title 'professional ethics'. Here we study the various ethical dilemmas which beset the complicated and difficult decisions made by the professionals. We should also evaluate the relevant policies. This approach can be called the narrow idea of professional ethics. Alternatively, we can call it a textbook approach.[5] Regardless of its merits we may also focus on the broader aspects of professional life, namely, its values and normative beliefs, both in the field of knowledge and action.

In this case we do not want to regulate professional practice. We are not trying to say what should or should not be done in certain problematic circumstances illustrated by dramatic case studies. For instance, should the doctor perform an abortion in the case of a very young girl who has been raped? This is an important problem. However, professional life provides a wider perspective on this same subject matter. We can now select health as the key medical goal and then ask whether the doctor's positive decision serves this goal. If it does not, the service ideal of doctors is jeopardized. The doctor aims at social justice and the mental welfare of the girl. Are such values also part of the package of the medical service ideal? Is the doctor professionally competent to judge the questions of justice? If he is not, he must rely on an external authority, and this endangers his claims to the monopoly of professional expertise in his own field. The acceptance of an external authority in the field of medicine threatens its professional role with a technical, engineering one. The doctors perform, at the same time as they suspend their own value judgements.

I cannot offer solutions to these problems in this paper. My sole purpose is to illustrate an alternative to the textbook approach to professional ethics. There is one additional bonus we can get from my broader philosophical approach. This is the possibility of first distancing ourselves from the modern or enlightenment view of the professions and then moving towards vaguely post-modern concerns. What this means is that the textbook approach must presuppose the usefulness of the ethical theories by means of which we judge the professional decisions and policies, just as we judge human action in general. We must also presuppose the existence of the science and authority of the professions.[6] This is a heavy package. It is a two dimensional, foundationalist theory, both ethically and sociologically.

When we adopt the broad view, everything changes. The ethical theories mentioned above are no longer needed, science can be criticized and the monopoly claims to authority repudiated. When we focus on the construction of professional achievements, a cynical perspective opens up and along with it the possibility of the criticism of the professions in a non-foundationalist manner. The main view in this case is that professions serve values which are simple and objective and possess scientific expertise. Of such values one wants to say only that they are as objective as socially possible. This much one must say because professions are justifiable in social life. It is part and parcel of their social existence that their service ideals cannot be questioned. Their life is a good one by definition.

III

To illustrate the broad approach to professional ethics we may compare engineering to such professions as medicine, law and education. Is engineering a profession in the same sense as the last mentioned classic professions are?

My answer will be in the negative. Engineering is a pseudo-profession. Such an answer will help us see some difficulties in engineering ethics in a realistic way. This in its turn may help engineers themselves to take a more realistic look at their own work and write their codes of ethics accordingly. But let us emphasize immediately that because we are not doing textbook professional ethics we are in no position to judge and condemn engineering decisions. If critical points emerge, they take the form of irony and an emerging cynicism. And because in the long run one cannot live with such attitudes, the engineering profession should accept the challenge and defend its ways. The result may be a better ethics for the future. Hence the broad approach represents genuine ethics in that it has its practical effects, unlike the purely sociological and descriptive approach.

Engineering has been called 'the profession that failed', whatever this slogan means. It can be taken to say that, compared to the classic professions, their service ideals and science, engineering is not quite the profession it has been taken to be. But certainly engineers have a fully efficient science at their disposal. Is there any question about their values? Hardly so, as can easily been seen:

> engineers are required to 'hold paramount the safety, health and welfare of the public,' to 'issue public statements only in an objective and truthful manner,' to 'act in professional matters for each employer or client as faithful agents and trustees,' and to 'avoid all conflicts of interest.' Each engineer stands to benefit from these requirements both as ordinary person and as engineer(Davis, 1991, p.158).

Once we know this much, it is natural to continue as follows:

> Imagine what engineering would be like if engineers did not generally act as the canons require. If, for example, engineers did not generally hold paramount the safety, health and welfare of the public, what would it be like to be an engineer? The day to day work would, of course, be much the same. But every now and then an engineer would be asked to do something that, though apparently profitable to his employer or client, would put other people at risk, some perhaps about whom he cared a great deal. Without a professional code, an

4

engineer could not object *as an engineer* (Davis, 1991, p. 158).

Michael Davis' point is that engineering is a true profession which has its own service ideal and a code of ethics based on this ideal. The key value words are safety, health and welfare.

But we need also to understand correctly the meaning of the word 'public'. Davis writes about this as follows:

> I would suggest that what makes people a public is their relative innocence, helplessness, or passivity. On this interpretation, 'public' would refer to those persons whose lack of information, technical knowledge, or time for deliberation renders them more or less vulnerable to the powers an engineer wields on behalf of his client or employer (Davis, 1991, pp.164-5).

This is to say that an engineer has her employer/client whose faithful agent and trustee she is. Then there is also the innocent and helpless member of the public who should be taken care of. For example, if an engineer builds a car, and he knows that it has an engine that is too powerful for the presently adopted suspension design he should tell the public about it. What happens then is almost a miracle: the public are transformed customers, whose own sole responsibility it is to make the purchase decision and bear the risks and expenses that follow from it. Because they know, they are no longer innocent or helpless, which is to say that they are not members of the public.

Of course in many cases it is impossible to turn the public into customers or other types of responsible users of engineering designs. Often people do not control the devices which influence the quality of their lives. A heating system may contain asbestos without anyone realizing this fact. Anyway, an engineer has her double role and personality. On the one hand she is a faithful agent and trustee and on the other, she has her responsibilities towards the innocent public.

Such a notion of engineering ethics makes engineering a classic profession whose central values, mentioned in their code of ethics, form their service ideal, which they fulfil by using their scientific expertise. I want to criticize this theory. Its user seems to provide a false testimony of professional life by dismissing the most important feature of what can be called the service ideal. Moreover, this criticism helps us to see better the place of values in the field of professional social organizations. The point is that the connection between values and professional activity is more complicated than one would like to think. In actual fact the connection is so deep that we may get suspicious of its reality even in the case of the classic professions.

IV

We need to elaborate on the claims made above. Figuratively speaking, engineering can be called 'material logic' in the sense that the content of its propositions is not mentioned. In other words, engineers produce what can be called efficient designs, regardless of what these designs are.[8] If they are moral engineers they feel responsible for the safety, health and welfare of the public, but these are side constraints, not the goals of the designs themselves.

Let us say that an engineer has his employer, and the employer's actions change the environment and life of people ('people' is understood as almost a technical term here). Some of the people form the public, namely, those who are innocent, helpless and passive. As I said, sometimes but not always members of the public can be changed into people. Engineers are responsible for the safety, health and welfare of the public, and this holds only for the public but not for people. This seems to make sense. Once you know that a design is risky, it is up to you to make the decision to use it. We can say that the responsibility of engineers for their own values is conditional on the existence of the public. In other words, the engineer's responsibility is strictly public relative. If there is no public, there is no responsibility. Then they may design anything.

Of course a Janus faced profession looks in the direction of the employer/client as well. Here the interesting and relevant point is that an employer/client is often himself a member of the public. If a car factory orders new tools and machines from an engineer it is first of all clear that the client cannot know about all the safety, health and welfare related features of the new designs. Thus a necessary condition for being a member of the public is fulfilled. Another necessary condition, which together with the first one is jointly sufficient, is the fact that the client's success is dependent on the new design. In other words, he is a user of the design.

It seems to follow from the moral norm stating that the engineer is a faithful agent and trustee of the client that he must inform his client about all the relevant aspects of the use of the design. But this is exactly how he should act towards those members of the public who are not his clients. We can insist that the engineer must be a trustee and a faithful agent of all the public. There is thus no difference between the client and the rest of the public.

However, such a conclusion seems to be far too strong. An engineer who acts as a faithful agent and trustee for all the public cannot serve her clients and employers. These are typically people who do not 'avoid all conflicts of interest' nor do they necessarily abstain from violations of such

6

values as public safety, health and welfare. They are interested in efficient designs and they see that the concept of efficiency does not logically entail safety, health and welfare. On the contrary, efficiency is related to (say) safety only if society enforces the relevant laws and regulations. Some unsafe cars have very efficient and successful designs. Laws are needed to protect people because they, and only they, create a connection between efficiency and safety, health and welfare. At the same time it is obviously true that engineers should keep their eye on these values as side constraints on their designs.

An engineer's client/employer may be a war-mongering state, corrupt secret police, a greedy businessman or a sloppy civil servant. The engineering task may be a bridge over a river in a location where it will certainly be useless. One's task may first involve designing weapons and then hospitals where the victims are treated. In fact there is no guarantee in engineering ethics that the client/employer is ethical in the sense required of engineers themselves. The value of being faithful to them becomes at best questionable.

We can now identify the following problem in engineering ethics. Engineers have their three values, safety, health and welfare, which they promote to the public. Clearly, this requirement is unproblematic when it applies to the client/employer, but it is problematic in the case of the rest of the public. The problem is created by the fact that the employer/client's goals and values may be in conflict with those of the rest of the public. For instance, when an engineer designs hand grenades, it is important that these are safe (they do not explode too early), and that they promote health (they kill the enemy that would otherwise kill you) and welfare (they are light to carry and easy to throw). But the grenades are not, and they cannot be, nice to the enemy, on the contrary. The more horrible they are, the more efficient is their design.

According to the above view of engineering ethics, it should be enough for the engineer to tell the enemy that the new hand grenades are really deadly. Then the victims do not belong to the category 'public', and the engineer is no longer responsible for the victims' suffering. It is up to the enemy if they want to take the risk and face the new danger.

Less cynically, one may want to suggest that such a dilemma faces only military, but not civil, engineers. Alas, this is not true. Civil engineers often serve clients/employers who are involved in what can be called exploitative conflicts so that the military dilemma is reproduced in civil life as well. It is important to focus on exploitation here, and not all possible conflicts, as we shall see.

For example, suppose an engineering company produces bugging devices for telephones and police radar detectors for cars. Both systems allow members of the public to exploit other people. The gadgets are designed to remain hidden so that the victim will go on doing what he is presently doing, thus revealing himself to the hidden observer. He can subsequently use the information at his disposal as he likes, most likely against the victim. Now if the engineer really cares about the welfare of the innocent and passive public, he should not produce such devices. If he cares only about the client and her safety and welfare, there is no ethical problem worth taking notice of. In terms of exploitative conflicts such an example seems to provide a line of argument against the common notion that engineering ethics should and can accommodate a universalized service ideal.

Values like safety, health and welfare are too broad and lofty to be used in the present context. This is not surprising because health is the key service ideal in medicine, just like welfare is in social work. Why and how should engineers invade the fields of these two classic professions? I do not see how this query could be answered in a satisfactory manner. Engineers cannot be experts in health and welfare. This follows from the contents of engineering curricula.

Suppose engineers design sewage systems. Certainly, this requires that health be taken into account throughout the design process. And if it is taken into account in an adequate manner, an engineer must know about health in this context. His knowledge, however, is adapted from sources that are outside the field of engineering. In fact, engineers must consult doctors. We can also say that engineering research and development does not produce a knowledge of health, although engineering utilizes such knowledge. Engineering alone is not enough if the central values of safety, health and welfare are to be fully recognized.

V

To understand the place of the service ideal in engineering and the classic professions like medicine, I want to suggest the following. In medicine the value 'health' is internal to the practice of the profession. In engineering the ideal value of the profession is external to the practice and work of the profession. This is to say that engineering is an example of a pseudo-profession. Its goals come from a source that is outside the profession and in this sense they are not the profession's own values (cf. side constraints).

An illustration of this is a new bridge that collapses. Though it was engineered, it was not an efficient design. A chemical compound that has no beneficial effect on the human body is not medicine. We do not know whether X is medicine before we know X works.

'Internal' is a word with many meanings and has a rather depressing history in idealistic philosophy, for instance in F.H.Bradley's metaphysics.

What is meant by this word here is simply that if a doctor works to undermine health, she does not work as a doctor but as an impostor and charlatan. Anyone who performs cosmetic plastic surgery is hard pressed to exploit the notion of health so that her activity fits it. If she cannot do that, her professional role is destroyed. Another example is a doctor working on athletes, trying to find new and undetectable methods of doping. Such a person is rather a medicine-man than a doctor, although he may well be using the latest and best techniques of scientific medicine.

Is this person now an engineer of the human body, aiming at an efficient design which is at the same time maximally safe, healthy and which promotes welfare, all this within the narrow bounds of the main goal, increased athletic performance? It is tempting to answer positively. This would also illustrate the meaning of 'external' in the context of practice and its values.

There is another way of putting the same point: in medicine scientific work constitutes the content of the concept of health. Health is not a theory free concept, as is easy to see. On the contrary, health is fully dependent on the present state of medical science and related professional practices.

Health used to connote a state without illness. In this sense it was possible for a person to be perfectly healthy, that is, not to be ill. It may be a rare condition, but it is possible. However, when the number of diseases grows and the classification of illnesses becomes so complicated that no one can hope to be healthy, under the traditional concept of health, 'health' changes its meaning.

Now a person is healthy in the comparative sense of being healthier than he used to be, healthier than the average person or healthier than could be expected, given his life context. No one can hope to be in perfect health. This is a doctor's dream since every one now stands in need of some kind of treatment. Every person can benefit from therapy that makes his life better, so that he is less likely to contract diseases and will live longer. Such a concept of health depends heavily on the doctor's knowledge of what benefits a person and what effects, if any, certain treatments have. The illness based notion was easier to apply since one can notice most diseases when one contracts one. But even here, if one wants to continue along Foucauldian lines, one may remark that the whole notion of disease is a theoretic-practical medical construction.[9] Without medicine, we are not ill. We just suffer and die.

What about engineers? One may well agree that health and welfare are external values in the engineering life. But what should be said about safety? This value may well be internal to engineering practice. More constructive suggestions however can be made in the present context. One may claim that the key, internal engineering value is expressed as follows:

Engineering aims at a good control over the artificial environment, where 'good' means safe, healthy and welfare promoting in a very broad sense.

It seems that any attempt to introduce internal values and ideals into engineering is bound to fail. Engineering and similar pseudo-professions are technical by nature. They deal with methods by means of which the client/employer can realize his own values, which may be embedded in professional or business goals.

For example, when I wash dishes in a restaurant, the rule is that I must not put broken glasses back into circulation. I must discard them. This is a safety regulation. But it is not true that I wash the dishes because of customer safety. Neither do I wash them in order to find broken glasses. And no one would claim that if a broken glass finds its way back to the tables, it is not washed. It can be perfectly clean but unsafe to use.

Another way of distinguishing between medicine and engineering is to use practical syllogisms,[10] first in medicine:

1. I believe the only way to stay healthy is to do X.
2. I want to be healthy.
3. Thus, I do X.

Next, we look at a practical syllogism in engineering:

1. I believe that the only way to build a bridge is to do Y.
2. I want to build a bridge.
3. Thus, I do Y.

When we look at the first syllogism, it is plain that one cannot reject the second premise, since I cannot fail to want to be healthy. Of course it may happen that I would like to be sick in order to avoid army conscription in an unjust war. But under normal conditions, the second premise is unavoidable. If the first premise is based on medical information, then we reach the conclusion logically.

The second syllogism is different. One can easily deny the second premise, since there is nothing compelling in it, simply because neither a bridge nor bridge building are value notions. A bridge may be a good device in certain situations and for certain purposes. But there are also normal situations where a bridge need not be built. Though we need a reason for building a bridge, we need no reason for being healthy.

The second syllogism is interesting mainly because of its first premise. This is what we should expect, if engineering is about efficient designs. When we unpack the first premise, we see that Y must contain a clause that refers at least to safety but perhaps also to health and welfare. If one wants to build a bridge, which is always questionable, one should do it as

10

the engineers say. This is equivalent of focusing on the first premise of the second syllogism.

VI

Whatever we design must be safe, or as safe as possible. But the concept of safety is not used in any universalized sense in engineering ethics. First of all, safety is relativized in relation to the concept of public. One must also keep in mind that nothing is ever designed for the sole purpose of making it safe. The object of design has its own purpose and use, in relation to which safety is also a desirable feature. The situation is different in medicine. Everything is done with health as the only goal. When one denies this, one adopts a cynical view of the professions. A similar attitude in engineering has nothing to do with cynicism. But the cynical view may well be the truth about the professions. At least in this sense engineering is innocent work.

If what has been said above has any value as a theory, what happens to engineering? It seems that engineering may profit from the above view. The reason is that engineers have suffered from unfair comparisons with the classic professions whose service ideal provides such a strong foundation for their practical authority. Engineers have been trying, obviously quite unsuccessfully, to answer the various charges against them. For example, the arms race, environmental pollution and the exploitation of natural resources, as well as many similar problems seem to involve the failure of engineers to fulfil the promise of their key values. But if engineers do not have any key values they cannot be accused of the relevant failures. They have simply done their best.

In this way engineers must make a choice between two alternatives, both of which may look rather uninviting. These are, first, to claim that they possess a service ideal, based on internal values, which they have been unsuccessful in realizing. Second, engineers may represent a technical pseudo-profession which serves other values than those of their own. As side constraints engineers should observe safety etc.

It seems that the second alternative is the reasonable choice. It allows engineers to distance themselves from the classic professions and choose the way that leaves them free to decide what to do, what values to support and what policies to realize. The first alternative is simply unrealistic.

Finally, a brief answer to the question of why engineers themselves and their audience try so hard to find an internal service ideal also in engineering. It is clear that engineering serves human welfare; that cannot be doubted. But such a remark is vacuous because all human action, if it is action, aims at welfare and presupposes freedom — as Alan Gewirth has so forcefully argued (Gewirth, 1978, pp.48ff.) Therefore, in this sense, the goal of engineering is human good, and engineering both as work and as a pseudo-profession has its undeniable worth. We need technical knowledge and the relevant means of realizing efficient designs. This is good, but it is a good that is different from the good promoted through the service ideals of the classic professions. They promote a good that is their own construction, or an internal good. Whether we should want such a professional monopoly over values is another thing.

Notes

1. For a comprehensive sociological account of professions, see Abbott, Andrew (1988), *The System of Professions,* University of Chicago Press, Chicago.
2. See, for example, Barnsley, John H. (1972), *The Social Reality of Ethics*, Routledge & Kegan Paul, London.
3. An excellent critical account of the professions is Wilding, Paul (1982), *Professional Power and Social Welfare*, Routledge & Kegan Paul, London.
4. See Grunbaum, Adolf (1984), *The Foundations of Psychoanalysis,* University of California Press, Berkeley.
5. For example, Appelbaum, David and Lawton, Sarah Verone (eds.), (1990) *Ethics and the Professions*, Prentice Hall, Englewood Cliffs, N.J. and Callahan, Joan C. (ed.), (1988) *Ethical Issues in Professional Life*, Oxford University Press, New York.
6. An interesting case is unnecessary medical treatment. See Paris, John J. and Reardon, Frank E. (1992), 'Physician refusal of requests for futile or ineffective interventions', *Cambridge Quarterly of Healthcare Ethics* vol. 1, no. 2, Spring, pp. 127-34..
7. See, for instance, Goldman, Alan H. (1980), *The Moral Foundations of Professional Ethics I, Rowman and Littlefield, Totowa, N.J.* pp. 8-9.
8. Polish praxiology takes this notion very seriously; see the articles in Gasparski, W. and Pszczolowski, T. (1983), *Praxiological Studies: Polish Contributions to the Science of Efficient Action*, Reidel, Dordrecht.
9. See Foucault, Michel (1965), *Madness and Civilization*, Vintage Books, New York.
10. See von Wright, G.H. (1971), *Explanation and Understanding*,Routledge and Kegan Paul, London, pp. 9 ff.

References

Davis, Michael (1991), 'Thinking like an engineer: the place of a code of ethics in the practice of a profession', *Philosophy and Public Affairs*, vol. 20, no. 2 Spring.

Gewirth, Alan (1978), *Reason and Morality*, University of Chicago Press, Chicago.

2 Medical education: Knowledge and know-how

K. W. M. Fulford

Introduction

The importance of education as an aspect of what constitutes a profession has been widely recognized (Calman and Downie, 1988). Professional training serves a number of functions. Most obviously, it imparts knowledge and skills. But it also transmits an ethos, a set of mores and practices by which the values of the profession in question are passed on to new entrants (Dyer, 1991).

The training offered by a professional body is thus a direct reflection of that profession's view of its own identity. This is generally left implicit in discussions of professional education, however. In this chapter, this will be illustrated for the case of medicine. We will look first at the way in which medical education has (by and large unreflectingly) adopted and, hence, perpetuated, an exclusively scientific model of the subject. We will find that this extends to medical education even in ethics. An alternative model of medicine will then be outlined in which there is a balance between the scientific and ethical aspects of the subject. This 'balance model' will in turn suggest a different approach to medical education, an approach which is the basis of an experimental course being set up in Oxford. Finally, some of the implications of a balance model for our understanding of the nature of medicine as a profession will be briefly considered.

Medical education and the medical model

The traditional 'medical model', as Ruth Macklin has pointed out, comes in a number of different versions (Macklin, 1973). The common feature of these models, however, is the idea that medicine is essentially a science.

Boorse has developed a detailed philosophical version of this scientific model of medicine (Boorse, 1975). A naive medical model would simply equate medicine with, say, biology: this model is behind much of the debate about mental illness (Fulford, 1989, ch 1); and it is openly espoused in the latest classifications of psychiatric disorders (American Psychiatric Association, 1987; Frances et al., 1991; and World Health Organisation, 1992). Boorse on the other hand acknowledges that medicine is not a purely scientific discipline. In medical practice, in particular, he points out, questions of value are inescapable; and this is reflected in the negatively value-laden nature of the patient's experience of illness. But behind this, he argues, there is a value-free body of scientific knowledge of disease, defined by reference to objective norms of bodily and mental functioning. This, then, is medical theory. This is what marks out the doctor's specifically medical area of expertise. This is what, in Boorse's view, divides medicine off from morals.

Medical education reflects a broadly Boorsean view of medicine. Since the publication of the Pond report, a growing number of medical schools are gradually introducing courses in ethics (Pond, 1987). But the syllabus, both preclinical and clinical, of most medical schools is still dominated by scientific subjects: in the preclinical course, medical students study anatomy, pharmacology, biochemistry, physiology, pathology and so forth; and then in the clinical years, they move on to cardiology, respiratory medicine, obstetrics, surgery, and other science-based medical specialities. It is recognized of course that know-how is important as well as knowledge, that as Weinstein (1993) has put it, medicine involves performative as well as epistemic expertise. But it is assumed that the know-how in question is limited largely to such essentially technical skills as auscultation, venesection and interpreting an X-ray.

Attention to the scientific basis of medicine is crucially important in medical education. The professions have sometimes been criticized for over-reliance on specialized scientific knowledge (Illich, 1977; McKee, 1991). And knowledge is, indeed, power in the doctor-patient relationship. Yet it is obviously essential that the doctor attending a child with, say, meningitis knows her bacteriology, neurology and pharmacology. And on a grander scale, the remarkable successes of scientific medical research in recent years can hardly be exaggerated.

Science is essential, then. Yet the critics of medicine are surely right if their point is directed against the way in which medical scientific knowledge has tended to be applied in practice. Medical knowledge has too often been used, not to empower the patient, but as a power base for the doctor. This has sometimes been for reasons which on any view are unprofessional — commercial gain, for instance, or merely to support a fragile ego. But more sinister has been the superficially benign paternalism of 'doctor knows best'. Acting from the best of professional motives, doctors, precisely as their scientific knowledge has increased, have used this as a platform from which to impose their values. Instead of a partnership, then, instead of shared decision making, the patients' views, experiences, wishes, and indeed their very understanding of their own illness, have all been marginalized. In short, the patient, in this relationship, has been treated as less than a person (Toombs, 1993).

Few doctors, nowadays, advocate paternalism, at any rate of the unbridled 'take it or leave it' variety. But that its dehumanizing influences are still there, more subtly, undermining the service the profession provides, is evident from the growing volume of complaints made by patients against doctors. These are in general concerned not with high-flown ethical failings but with a lack of ordinary human consideration, such as not giving sufficient time, failure to pay attention, insensitivity and even plain rudeness (Cleary and McNeil, 1988). It is as though, as our knowledge of the scientific basis of medicine has increased, so our ability to treat our patients as people has diminished.

As an overview this is of course grossly unfair to all those individual doctors who provide a first class service at a human as well as technical and scientific level. But the pattern of complaints shows that it is not an unfair picture of the way in which the profession as a whole is perceived by those it serves. And this indeed is hardly surprising given the training doctors receive. The anatomy they study at the very outset of their induction into the profession of medicine is not living anatomy. Medical students normally 'cut their teeth', as it were, on the cadaver. Their first experience of medical training is dissecting the dead body. This is followed by decerebrate cats, isolated frogs' legs jumping to electric shocks, foetuses in pathology pots, and other experiences seemingly designed to dehumanize the experience of medicine.

As they progress to their clinical training, medical students, by definition, start to see patients. Here, it might be expected, the balance between the technical and personal, the scientific and human, should start to be redressed. Students are indeed exposed to role models of good patient care. This is the traditional means by which the skills of applying medical knowledge are acquired, through apprenticeship, through observation of more experienced colleagues under supervision. This is certainly essential to the development of good clinical skills. It is, perhaps, recognized that apprenticeship alone will no longer be sufficient as we face the new challenges of artificial prolongation of life, genetic medicine, control of fertility and the like (Hope and Fulford, 1993). But here, it may be said, medicine, in partnership with philosophy, has already responded by inventing bioethics, a subject which is already at least on the agenda of medical education.

16

Paradoxically, though, it is precisely here, in bioethics, that the continuing dominance of an essentially scientific medical model is most clearly seen. This is evident at both practical and theoretical levels. At a practical level it is evident in the continuing marginalization of medical ethics in 'the curriculum. Ethics is generally taught by non-medics — lawyers, theologians, philosophers. The teaching provided is excellent. But from the student's perspective, the fact that it is not provided by a clinician inevitably makes it seem peripheral to the requirements of good clinical care. Similarly, the time given to the subject is usually highly restricted. Often attendance is not even compulsory. Only rarely is the subject examined. All in all, then, the impression is of a sop to public opinion, time grudgingly spared from the serious business of clinical training, with an imported teacher placed in the invidious role of the 'token ethicist'.

At a theoretical level the dominance of a scientific model of medicine is evident in the self-constructs of bioethics itself (Fulford, 1993a). This is perhaps more surprising, that bioethicists themselves collude in a model of medicine in which science is at the centre and ethics only at the periphery. Yet a transparent illustration of this is the focus in bioethics on problems of treatment rather than diagnosis. The picture is of a value-free assessment of the problem, using scientific tools of diagnosis, with values coming in only when a decision has to be made about treatment. This is understandable to the extent that bioethics emerged originally as a response to the challenges posed by 'high tech' medicine. But taking medicine as a whole, in primary care as well as in hospital practice, it is clear that questions of value can also be important at the stage of diagnosis (Reich, 1991). What is to count as a problem; what is to count as a medical problem; what aspects of a medical problem are of concern; all these are questions which in part turn on the way in which the condition of the patient is evaluated. Yet even those bioethicists who recognize this still persist in drawing a distinction between ethical and medical considerations. Beauchamp and Childress, for instance, emphasize that judgements of irrationality (in psychiatry) are heavily value laden. But what they conclude from this is not that medical diagnoses involve value judgements. It is rather that judgements of rationality involve, in their words, 'moral *rather than* medical considerations' (Beauchamp and Childress, 1989, p.84, my emphasis).

So long, then, as ethics is marginalized even in bioethics, it must remain marginalized in the medical self-image, and hence in medical education. This could be right. If the scientific medical model is correct, then it *is* right. So the question arises, is the scientific medical model correct?

17

A balance model of the medical concepts

This brings us to recent philosophical work setting out an alternative model of the concepts of illness and disease, one in which scientific (or descriptive) and ethical (or evaluative) considerations are given equal weight. I will not attempt to review this work in detail here. However there are three features of the model, each of them 'balancing-up' features, which are directly relevant to medical education.

The first balancing-up feature is between fact and value, or description and evaluation, themselves. If we look carefully at how the medical concepts are actually used, it is clear that they are in part evaluative, rather than, as the scientific medical model would suggest, purely descriptive in nature (Agich, 1983; Fulford, 1989, ch.3; Nordenfelt, 1987). This conclusion has been taken to undermine the authority of medical science. The critics of psychiatry have made this explicit. Szasz, for instance, takes his observation that the concept of mental illness is value-laden to show that it is not really illness at all, and hence that psychiatry borrows an illegitimate authority from physical medicine (Szasz, 1960). A balance model, on the other hand, has quite different implications. Rather than rejecting the scientific medical model, rather than replacing it with an ethical model, it produces a balance of the two. It shows that fact and value, description and evaluation, are woven together as warp and weft in the conceptual structure of medicine as a whole, in physical medicine as well as in psychological, and in high tech hospital medicine as well as in primary care (Fulford, 1989).

If illness and disease are value terms, however, they are not value terms simpliciter — being ill or having a disease is different from, say, being wicked or ugly. Analysis of the particular kind of value expressed by the medical concepts leads to a second balancing-up feature, between illness and disease. In the Boorse-type scientific medical model, the concept of disease is logically primary (Boorse, 1975). This corresponds with the paternalistic use of medical knowledge of disease to devalue the patient's experience of illness (Fulford and Hope, 1993). But once both disease and illness are seen to be value terms, it is illness, not disease, which is found to be logically primary (Fulford, 1989, ch.5). The relationship between illness and disease is complex. But the logical primacy of illness arises essentially from the fact that it is the patient's experience of illness which, ultimately, marks out a change in bodily structure and functioning as a disease, not vice versa.

This of course raises the question, how is the patient's experience of illness defined? Here a third balancing-up feature of the model becomes important. Again, without going into the details, the line of argument runs thus. The experience of illness consists, centrally, in incapacity, and

18

incapacity means failure of action or loss of agency. Thus where the concept of disease is most naturally analyzed (as by Boorse) in terms of disturbance of functioning, the experience of illness is naturally analyzed in terms of failure of action. But action, in this sense, is a property of persons. As Toulmin has pointed out, patients are indeed patients to the extent that they are no longer agents (Toulmin, 1980). Hence in a balance model of the medical concepts, the bodily and mental parts and systems, which are the focus of the scientific medical model, are balanced by the actions of the patient as a person (Fulford, 1989, ch.7).

In this balance model, then, values, the experiential aspects of illness, and the patient as a person, are all as important as the facts, disease theories, and disturbances of functioning emphasized in an exclusively scientific medical model. This in turn implies the need for a different model of medical education.

The Oxford Practice Skills course

The Oxford Practice Skills course is a practical counterpart in medical education to the balance model of the medical concepts (Fulford and Hope, 1993). The course has three main elements, ethics, law and communication skills, corresponding broadly with the three balancing-up features of the conceptual model. First, ethics connects directly with the evaluative logical element of the model — if value judgements are integral to medical diagnosis as well as to treatment, a sensitivity to the evaluative aspects of a case, and an ability to reason ethically, are essential clinical skills. Second, communication skills in medicine turn crucially on an understanding of the patient's experience of illness. Third, much at least of medical law turns specifically on the loss of agency or capacity involved in 'failure of action' — this is most transparently true of mental health law, much of which explicitly involves issues of capacity, but it is true also of the broader protections which the law in general extends to the patient in the doctor-patient relationship.

The central idea behind the Practice Skills course is thus that these three elements — ethics, communication skills and the law — should be taught in a fully integrated package with the scientific and technical aspects of clinical training. The rationale for this is that just as the corresponding logical elements are all interwoven together in the concepts of illness and disease, so the elements of practice skills are all interwoven together in day-to-day clinical work.

Consider the following case:

A 55 year old man has valvular heart disease causing breathlessness on mild exertion. He might benefit from surgery, but the surgery has risks, and the results are not certain. The surgeon nonetheless believes that an operation would be worthwhile. How should he proceed?

Here the patient's consent is an important legal defence to battery, reflecting the fundamental ethical principle of autonomous patient choice; but establishing consent, as opposed to mere assent, involves, among other things, complex communication skills such as exploring the patient's fears and wishes, explaining the risks and benefits in a meaningful way, and so on. And this in turn depends among other things on a sound knowledge of the basic medical facts.

In our practice skills seminars, then, we start from problematic clinical situations such as these and work back to the practice skills required to deal with them effectively.

The course has a number of other features which we believe are innovative and which are designed to integrate the elements of practice skills — ethics, law and communication skills — into the everyday clinical thinking of the students: first, instead of a separate 'block' or module, it takes the form of a series of seminars spread right through the three years of the clinical course; second, each seminar focuses on a topic relevant to the students' current clinical work - consent, for instance, is covered during surgery; third, wherever possible the seminars are taught jointly by the practice skills team (which includes philosophers) together with the clinical teachers on the firm to which the students are attached at the time; and fourth, appraisal of the student's practice skills is included as an integral part of their overall clinical assessment.

The Practice Skills course is experimental and it is still too early to comment in detail on its effectiveness. However the feedback from students and from a majority of doctors is encouraging. The question arises, then, what are the implications of the model for our understanding of what it is to be a professional.

Practice skills and the professional

The nature of a profession has been widely debated (Davis, 1991; Downie, 1990). Here I want to note just three points arising specifically from the model of medicine and medical education outlined above. The first point is that although different professional groups have different knowledge bases, there are a number of common factors involved in good

20

professional practice. The importance of ethics, law and communication skills, in particular, is not limited to the practice of medicine. Similar practice skills are important in nursing, physiotherapy and other health care professions, and indeed beyond health care in law, accountancy, engineering and the like. Practice skills, then, in virtue of their generality, are, perhaps, of the essence of what it is to be a professional, regardless of profession. Certainly this would be consistent with attempts in the literature to define the essence of what it is to be a professional by reference to particular norms of good conduct (Goldman, 1980).

By the same token, though, good practice skills might be thought not to be specific even to the professions, at least as generally understood. There is an ethics of coal mining surely, and certainly no shortage of mining law; and good communication skills must be essential to safe working conditions at the coal face. And in one sense this analysis does indeed bridge the gap between professions and other occupations. However this is because practice skills — as defined here — are essential to relationships between people. Mining and doctoring both involve other people. Hence mining and doctoring, alike, can be pursued in an ethical or unethical way, are carried on within a framework of law, and necessarily involve inter-personal communication.

The difference, though, to come to the second point, is that doctoring involves people essentially. Mining could be done by robots for robots and would still be mining. Medicine, even if fully automated, would still be concerned with people. This may seem a trivial observation. But remember that behind much of the dissatisfaction with modern scientific medicine is a tendency to dehumanize the patient. The practice skills model, then, is consistent with what Downie has called 'service through relationship' as a mark of the professional (Downie, 1990). There is room here for a variety of different 'service relationships', of course — the 'professional-as-parent', the paternalistic model still so prevalent in medicine; but also the 'merchant-professional', selling her knowledge and skills; and the 'professional-as-partner', working in an equal relationship of mutual respect. A given relationship may be more appropriate to one profession than another, and indeed at one time compared with another. In medicine, perhaps, although 'consumer choice' is more important than it was (Brody, 1987); we are perhaps in danger of stepping too far towards a merchant-relationship (Sulmsay, 1993). But the common factor remains a relationship of service as the mark of the professional.

If this is the mark of the professional in general, though, what is there left to mark out the medical professional in particular? Are we back with a traditional medical model after all, one in which the scope of specifically medical expertise is defined by reference to an exclusively scientific knowledge base?

In a balance model of the medical concepts, however, as we saw earlier, it is not merely value simpliciter which is important, but specifically medical value. It is by this that illness is marked off from other negative evaluative concepts such as wickedness and ugliness. My third point, then, is that evaluative considerations may come into what might be called, adapting Searle (1969), the constitutive as well as the regulative rules of a profession, that is the rules by which a profession is defined as well as those by which good practice is governed.

This is the most speculative of the three points. Most commentators have argued that a professional is identified, inter alia, by expertise in relation to a particular knowledge base. As we saw earlier, this is the essence of the 'medical' model of disease. Davis (1991) has argued that the mark of the professional (whether in the traditional professions or in areas normally thought of as trades) is that she justifies her advice primarily by referring to her particular area of technical knowledge. And in the courts, consistently, the professional called as an expert is assumed to be 'a man of science', an expert to the facts.

The practice skills model of the professional, implying as it does that the constitutive as well as regulative features of a profession are value laden, is thus radically at odds with the standard view. Yet it is not a far-fetched model. We noted earlier the wide range of arguments supporting the view that the medical concepts, disease and illness, are value concepts. Legal concepts, more obviously even than medical, are value laden, either directly (e.g. malice aforethought, mens rea) or indirectly (i.e., by way of the notion of intent). And the defining concepts of accountancy (profit and loss, valuation, money itself) are all transparently value laden.

Our third point, then, if speculative, is not far-fetched. It is also the most significant point. It is significant, first, for our understanding of the nature of the professional. We noted a moment ago that Downie's notion of 'service through relationship' links the professional essentially to people. The coal miner is concerned essentially with coal; the astronomer is concerned essentially with stars. Coal miners and astronomers, that is to say, however professional they may be in other senses of the term, are not, like healthcare workers, lawyers or accountants, concerned essentially with people. But value systems attach paradigmatically to persons (and animals). Hence to the extent that the professional is concerned essentially with persons, it should come as no surprise to find that their areas of expertise are constituted by evaluative as well as factual considerations.

The point is also significant though for the regulative aspects of professionalism. The standard model encourages paternalism. The professional is an expert to a body of knowledge which she dispenses to her client. True, the professional should dispense her knowledge beneficently, with the 'best interests' of her client in mind. But the model

22

of a value-free body of specialist knowledge inevitably carries with it a picture of what Alderson (1990) has called an 'ignorant and (hence) dependant laity'. This has all too often been the corollary of the standard medical model. But it is a model which is no longer sustainable once it is recognized that considerations of value come into the concepts by which the professional's area of expertise is defined. In many cases these considerations are unproblematic and hence can be ignored. This is the case with many diseases, for instance (Fulford, 1989, ch.4). But in psychiatry and in a number of areas of primary health care, considerations of value may be highly problematic (Fulford, Smirnoff and Snow, 1993). In such cases, therefore, attention to the patient's wishes and values is integral to the professional's expert assessment as well as to their advice on treatment.

Recognizing the importance of an evaluative element in the constitutive as well as regulative rules of medicine as a profession has implications for phenomenology (Fulford, 1993b) and disease classification (Fulford, 1994a) as well as for ethics (Fulford, Smirnoff and Snow, 1993). These are bought at a price, however. For the practice skills model implies that in some sense the professional must be an expert on values as well as facts (Fulford, 1994b). This of course is not to say that the task of the professional is to determine questions of value. But to be sensitive to such questions, to recognize them as they arise, to be aware of their implications, and to have the skills to work successfully with patients and other professionals whose values may be different from one's own, all these become essential to the professional's role.

And it is this, finally, which brings in the philosopher. For although a variety of disciplines are relevant to the evaluative aspects of medicine (sociology, psychology, religion, for instance), it is the philosopher, rather than the scientist, who is the expert at least on the logic of value terms and of related normative concepts such as action. It is, perhaps, a further reflection of the continuing dominance of the scientific medical model that philosophers have been almost wholly excluded even from such obviously conceptual areas of medicine as classification and diagnosis (Fulford, 1994a). But if the model presented here turns out to be right, philosophers will inevitably be drawn back in. For the ability of the doctor as a professional to serve the interests of her patients will increasingly be seen to depend as much on better understanding of the evaluative logical element in medicine, in both its constitutive and regulative aspects, as on further expansion of its scientific knowledge base.

Conclusions

In this article it has been argued that the training offered by a professional body is a direct reflection of that profession's view of its own nature and objectives. Medical education reflects the strongly scientific self-image of the subject in being occupied almost exclusively with the sciences basic to medicine. A sound training in these sciences is essential to good clinical practice, but in concentrating on the knowledge base of medicine, medical education has neglected the skills necessary for the successful application of that knowledge in individual cases. An alternative model of medical education being developed in Oxford has been described. In this model, ethics, law and communication skills (collectively 'practice skills') are brought together in a case-based approach to clinical training. This 'practice skills' approach reflects a model of the medical concepts in which the descriptive and scientific aspects of medicine are fully balanced by the evaluative and ethical. Some of the implications of this 'balance model' for our understanding of the nature of medicine as a profession have been briefly reviewed, in particular the way in which it shows the importance of evaluative considerations in the constitutive as well as regulative aspects of the subject.

Acknowledgements

I am grateful to Professor Ruth Chadwick for her helpful comments on an early draft of this paper.

Reference List

Agich, G.J. (1983), 'Disease and value: a rejection of the value-neutrality thesis', *Theoretical Medicine*, 4, pp. 27-41.

Alderson, P. (1990), 'Choosing for children: parents' consent to surgery', Oxford University Press New York, 193, pp. 203-4, 207.

American Psychiatric Association (1987), *Diagnostic and Statistical Manual of Mental Disorders*, Third edition, revised, American Psychiatric Association, Washington DC.

Beauchamp, T.L., Childress, J.F. (1989), *Principles of Biomedical Ethics,* Oxford University Press, Oxford.

Boorse, C. (1975), 'On the distinction between disease and illness', *Philosophy and Public Affairs vol.* 5, pp. 49-68.

Brody, B. (1987), 'Justice and competitive markets', *Journal of Medicine and Philosophy*, 12, pp. 37-50.

24

Calman, K.C. & Downie, R.S. (1988), 'Education and training in medicine', *Medical Education*, vol. 22, pp. 488-91.

Cleary, P.D. & McNeil, B.J. (1988), 'Patient satisfaction as an indicator of quality of care', *Inquiry*, vol. 25, pp. 25-36.

Davis, J.K. (1991), 'Professions, trades and the obligation to inform', *Journal of Applied Philosophy*, vol. 8, no. 2, pp. 167-76.

Downie, R.S. (1990), 'Professions and professionalism', *Journal of Philosophy of Education*, vol. 24, no. 2, pp. 147-59.

Dyer, A. (1991), 'Psychiatry as a profession', Ch.5 in Bloch, S. & Chodoff, P. (eds.) *Psychiatric Ethics*, Oxford Medical Publications, Oxford.

Frances, A., First, M.B., Widger, T.A., Miele, G.M., Tilly, S.H., Davis, W.W. & Pincus, H.A. (1991), 'An A-Z guide to DSM-IV conundrums', *Journal of Abnormal Psychology*, vol. 100 no. 3, pp. 407-12.

Fulford, K.W.M. (1989), *Moral Theory and Medical Practice*. Cambridge University Press.

Fulford, K.W.M. (1991), 'The concept of disease', Ch. 6 in Bloch, S. and Chodoff, P. (eds.) *Psychiatric ethics* (second edition). Oxford University Press, Oxford.

Fulford, K.W.M. (1993a), 'Bioethical blind spots: four flaws in the field of view of traditional bioethics', *Health Care Analysis*, vol. 1, pp. 155-62.

Fulford, K.W.M. (1993b), 'Thought insertion and insight: disease and illness paradigms of psychotic disorder', in Spitzer, M., Uehlein, F., Schwartz, M.A. & Mundt, C., (eds.), *Phenomenology, Language and Schizophrenia*. Springer-Verlag, New York.

Fulford, K.W.M. (1994a), 'Closet logics: hidden conceptual elements in the DSM and ICD classifications of mental disorders', in Sadler, J.Z., Schwartz, M., Wiggins, O., (eds.), *Philosophical Perspectives on Psychiatric Diagnostic Classification*, Johns Hopkins University Press.

Fulford, K.W.M. (1994b). 'Value, action, mental illness and the law', in Gardner, K., Horder, J. & Shute, S. (eds), *Criminal Law: Action, Value and Structure*, Oxford University Press, Oxford.

Fulford, K.W.M., Smirnoff, A.Y.U., Snow, E. (1993), 'Concepts of disease and the abuse of psychiatry in the USSR', *British Journal of Psychiatry*, vol. 162, pp. 801-10.

Fulford, K.W.M. & Hope, R.A. (1993), 'Psychiatric ethics: a bioethical ugly duckling?' in Gillon, R. (ed.), *Principles of Health Care Ethics*, John Wiley and Sons.

Goldman, A.H. (1980), *The Moral Foundations of Professional Ethics*, Totowa: Rowman and Littlefield.

Hope, R.A. & Fulford, K.W.M. (1993), 'Medical education: patients, principles and practice skills', in Gillon, R. (ed) *Principles of Health Care Ethics*. John Wiley and Sons.

Illich, I. (1977), *Limits to Medicine*, Pelican, Harmondsworth.

Macklin, R. (1973), 'The medical model in psychoanalysis and psychotherapy', *Comprehensive Psychiatry*, vol. 14, no. 1, pp. 49-69.

McKee, C. (1991), 'Breaking the mould: a humanistic approach to nursing practice', Ch. 8 in McMahon, R. & Pearson, A. (eds.). *Nursing as Therapy*, Chapman and Hall, London.

Nordenfelt, L. (1987), *On the nature of health: an action-theoretic approach*, D. Reidel Publishing Company, Dordrecht, The Netherlands.

Pond, D. (1987), *Report of a Working Party on the Teaching of Medical Ethics*, IME Publications Ltd, London.

Reich, W. (1991), 'Psychiatric diagnosis as an ethical problem', Ch. 7 in Bloch, S. & Chodoff, P., *Psychiatric Ethics* (second edition), pp 101-35. Oxford University Press, Oxford

Searle, J.R. (1969), *Speech Acts: An Essay in the Philosophy of Language*, Cambridge University Press, Cambridge.

Sulmasy, D.P. (1993), 'What's so special about medicine', *Theoretical Medicine*, vol. 14, pp. 27-42.

Szasz, T.S. (1960), 'The myth of mental illness', *American Psychologist*, vol. 15, pp. 113-18.

Toombs, S.K. (1993), *The Meaning of Illness: A Phenomenological Account of the Different Perspectives of Physician and Patient*, Kluwer Academic Publishers, Dordrecht, The Netherlands.

Toulmin, S. (1980), 'Agent and patient in psychiatry', *International Journal of Law and Psychiatry*, vol.3, pp. 267-78.

Weinstein, B.D. (1993), 'What is an expert?', *Theoretical Medicine*, vol. 14, pp. 57-73.

World Health Organisation (1992), *Mental Disorders: Glossary and Guide to Their Classification in Accordance with the Tenth Revision of the International Classification of Diseases*, WHO, Geneva, Switzerland.

3   Moral philosophy – another 'disabling profession?'

Jenneth Parker

1. Introduction

> Given philosophy's traditional concern with self-knowledge, philosophers' overwhelming lack of attention to and acceptance of the professional and institutional contexts of their own work is striking. (Stuhr, 1989)

Applied philosophy has been at the forefront of many developments which have brought philosophy into a fruitful relation to social problems and has made an unanswerable case for philosophy's social role. What could then be more natural or welcome than social recognition of the value of this role in the form of invitations to philosophers to serve on expert committees on matters of social importance? Initially I was pleased to see the increasing incidence of moral philosophers on 'expert committees', but these feelings gave way to concern as I began to consider the implications of this practice for philosophy. Part of this unease is caused by the 'expert' paradigm which I will examine more fully. Overall my concern resolved itself into the question can philosophers serve on expert committees and still uphold philosophical values?

This concern is shared by others, for example Don Marquis in his 'The role of Applied Ethics in Philosophy' sketches a possible and uncomfortable scenario where philosophers who produce ethics that suit hospital administrators are those who will be financially successful (Marquis, 1990). Equally, in the same way as we are rightly concerned about medical paternalism we must consider the possibility that philosophers could practise an ethical paternalism which could strike at the heart of philosophy as a critical social enterprise. That these issues should arise is no reflection on the probity of those involved in applied philosophy, it is obvious that if philosophy becomes directly involved in public affairs philosophers will become subject to pressures and dilemmas that are familiar to other professions. Professional ethics represent, at least in part, the attempt to face up to these pressures and give them analytical attention. A pragmatic reason for getting clear about the professional ethics of philosophy is that it is invidious to be in the position of commenting on the ethics of other professions when one's own profession is left unexamined.

Criticism of applied philosophy has come from those philosophers who believe the philosophical tradition is being undermined. My argument locates applied philosophy within the wider philosophical tradition with some consequences for the social assessment of the way that tradition serves or fails to serve the public. This is, therefore a general thesis about the values of philosophy as a profession applied to the particular case of philosophers on expert committees. It is appropriate that an inquiry into the professional ethics of philosophy should be undertaken from within applied philosophy itself as the question of professionalism implies engagement with social problems. However, I will argue that the whole of philosophy has a professional relationship to society which is closely related to the values of philosophy.

I introduce some general criticisms of professionalisation from Ivan Illich and go on to present aspects of both the Warnock report and the European report on bioethics as showing cause for concern. I then consider the sociological account of the professions and professional ethics and relate this to philosophy. I present an account of the general role of philosophy in the community and argue against substantive interpretations of moral expertise. I then draw some conclusions regarding expert committees and the need for further investigation of the professional ethics of philosophy.

2. Illich and the 'disabling professions'[1]

Ivan Illich and his school developed a polemical critique of the disabling role of the professions in society. Illich considered that the professions were taking over the role of theology as arbiters of the right way to live. This situation is implicitly contrasted with an ideal of civil democracy where community assessment must replace the current expert assessment. The critique focuses on two aspects; professional expertise as anti-democratic and the professional exceeding of expert remit.

Professional expertise as anti-democratic

'The public acceptance of domineering professions is essentially a political event. Each new establishment of professional legitimacy means that the political tasks of law-making, judicial review and executive power lose some of their proper character and independence. Public affairs pass from the lay person's elected peers into the hands of a self-crediting élite.' Here Illich is stressing the impoverishment of political debate that can result from a wrong use of professional expertise by government. He also wishes to stress the paternalism of expert opinion, stating that experts will typically try to decide what the public ought to do or ought to have without feeling the need for direct consultation. 'Government by a congress that bases its decisions on expert opinions, given by professions might be government for, but never by the people.'

Exceeding the remit

Illich complains that professionals are exceeding their professional competence and becoming ideologues. 'Professionals tell you what you need and claim the power to prescribe. They not only recommend what is good, but actually ordain what is right.' This is contrasted with a previous, more satisfactory state of affairs where the expert presented a circumscribed opinion to the limit of competence and people were expected to make up their own minds. Illich draws this example from the situation of an expert witness in a court of law and does not explicitly describe the way this might operate in society. However, the moral is clear — experts should stick to their own clearly defined area of competence and not stray into making prescriptions. This view is widely supported by other writers on the professions, for example Michael Bayles, 'The decision to adopt a program ... is a value judgement for which professionals have no more training than particular clients or the public. Thus, these decisions are for the public, either at large or their democratically elected representatives' (Bayles, 1981). Is it reasonable to hold that moral philosophers are outside of this judgement because the object of their inquiry is value?

3. Cause for concern? Warnock and the European bioethics report

In considering the two documents I will be using them primarily as examples of particular structural features of the operation of expert committees and not considering their particular recommendations in detail except where these bear on the structural relationship of the committees to society.

The Warnock report is the report of a committee of inquiry into human fertilisation and embryology set up by the British government in 1984. This report exemplifies some of the problems with expert committees which are required to make recommendations, it also exemplifies some of Illich's criticisms.

There is no explicit reflection on the role or remit of the committee itself in the report. We are told that 'Members of the Inquiry were reluctant to appear to dictate on matters of morals to the public at large. Equally they believed it was their task to attempt to discover the public good in the widest sense, and to make recommendations in the light of that ....' In this respect then, the committee overcame their reluctance to dictate on morals. Whilst claiming to base recommendations on argument no sentiment the findings do not present arguments for the judgements made — they are represented as global opinions as criticized in Illich.

The report shows a worrying lack of awareness of the inherent limitations of expert committee work. For example the relationship of the committee's work to already existing legal structures and laws. Warnock seems to take it for granted that consistency with extant law is a value in itself on the grounds that 'the law itself is the embodiment of a common moral position.' This raises the interesting possibility of a regressive justification as it is quite possible that most extant law has also been developed by expert committees. Obviously the terms of reference of a committee may not allow consideration of the validity or moral value of existing laws — but this should surely be clarified. As a minimum one would hope to see some account of the extant laws which are adjacent to, or set the context for, the topic under consideration. It may be part of the proper task of such a committee to comment on the adequacy or otherwise of such laws.

Mary Warnock makes it clear in her preamble that she is chairing this committee as a philosopher and employing her philosophical skills in so doing, though she does not detail what she believes are the appropriate philosophical skills in this context. She does quote an unnamed philosopher's phrase when she talks of the task of the committee as being to adopt a 'steady and general point of view.' However, many philosophers would want to question whether the task of philosophy is to articulate such a view, especially if it comes with an additional claim to social and political validity. Overall, the lack of any explicit reflection on the nature, constitution and validity of the committee itself is a worrying omission when the chair has achieved eminence in a profession priding itself on reflexive assessment.

This document, produced by the Council of Europe, is the report of a symposium on Bioethics in Europe which had the aim of promoting the European moral community through discussion and harmonized legislation. The report also contains the results of a questionnaire survey sent to 27 member states of which 23 replied.

The survey shows ethics committees to be widespread at national, regional and local levels. Committees are at present overwhelmingly consultative, but clinical trails committees in one-third of countries have decision-making powers. The jobs given to ethics committees include 'drawing up and development of guidelines, the giving of advice to the government or parliament, functioning as an appeals board, consultative work on difficult cases, training and information.' Appointment is most often directly by government in the case of national committees, whereas regional and local committees are appointed either by health authorities or by the institution themselves. This last point raises problems of independence of committees chosen by hospitals. Finally we are told that the fact that court action seldom results 'illustrates the efficiency of the practice of ethics engendered by ethics committees.' This shows a level of faith in informal regulation by experts which Illich would recognise as symptomatic of disabling professions at work in society.

It is envisaged that ethics committees will become increasingly important. For example consideration by an ethics committee is proposed as a legal condition for licensing procedures carried out on human embryos. This proposal states that 'experts in ethics' should be part of such a legally binding committee, indeed this phrase recurs throughout the report and is not challenged by any of the participants.

Concern is expressed in the report for the necessity of public involvement in bioethical debate, but no new mechanisms are suggested to facilitate this. It was stated that one aim of teaching bioethics is 'to promote social dialogue ... and to establish mechanisms for democratic decision-making.' Further emphasis on bioethics as a process came in consideration of the teaching of bioethics which ... serves to develop and strengthen the ethical conscience of those who work in the health sector and of the organisations they represent. One participant considered it necessary that committees should be aware of their obligation to inform the general community and it was suggested that the Council of Europe should make its findings more accessible and have public hearings.

4. The sociological account of the professions [4]

In this section I will take the sociological definitions of the professions as my starting point and go on to briefly outline a sociological account of professional responsibilities. I claim that philosophy can plausibly be regarded as a profession and justify this in section 5.

Before proceeding I must note a certain unease with the unreflecting acceptance of the concept of the 'professions' and 'professional ethics'. This unease derives from the impression given that no other kinds of work have a legitimate relation to ethical concerns. Against this devaluing of work I cite considerations of sustainability, which suggest that everyone needs to be aware of the ethical aspects of environmental impacts of their work (NIACE, 1993). However, whilst the whole question of ethics and work will repay philosophical attention, what makes the question of the professions urgent is their social power over individuals and communities. The fact that applied philosophy currently concentrates on articulation and discussion of the ethical codes of only certain kinds of work is both a manifestation and a recognition of that power.

There is much disagreement amongst sociologists as to the exact defining characteristics of professions, but the following are generally held to be required.

1. Professions provide services that require extensive intellectual training which is provided by recognised institutions. A distinction is usually made between the consulting professions and the scholarly professions on the grounds that the scholarly professions do not usually have a client group. I will return to this point later in connection with philosophy.

2. Professions typically exercise self-regulation and have a significant degree of autonomy. The extent of professionalisation can be equated with the extent of the social mandate achieved by the profession for defining the terms of its own operation.

3. Professions are relatively well paid for exercising the professional skills and judgement for which autonomy is required.

4. A broad perspective is that an occupational group develops certain self perceptions and convinces outsiders to accept its self image. Hence it accomplishes profession in interaction (Cotterell, 1982).

The following sections are sociological attempts to describe general features of the ideology of professionalism. From a sociological point of view codes of ethics can be considered as part of professional ideology, not necessarily in any negative sense.

The ideal of objectivity. There is a professional ideal of disinterestedness which is related to the intellectual task of systematizing cases from an intellectual base. Intellectually one aspect of a profession is a certain equilibrium between the universal and the particular (Hughes, 1963). Equally 'the professional is expected to think objectively and enquiringly about matters which may be for laymen, subject to orthodoxy or sentiment which limit intellectual exploration' (Hughes, 1963). The ideal of objectivity is related to the idea of general public service of the profession as a whole which is sometimes difficult to reconcile with client representation.

Self-regulation and reform. The legitimation of professional freedom depends upon a plausible exercise of self-regulation. Codes of practice and ethics form the ideological aspect of self-regulation and are designed to communicate important aspects of the self-definition of the profession both to the public and to initiates. Codes also proclaim the wider ideals of social responsibility, balancing these claims against the monopolistic power of the professions. Responsibility can extend to the ways that research may be used, and there is a tendency at present to take this type of responsibility more seriously. There exist pressure groups for this kind of reform in many of the professions (e.g. 'Scientists for Social Responsibility'). A functionalist analysis stresses the social bargain of professions — they are given a social mandate because of the beneficial effects they are believed to have on society. If a profession is not seen to be delivering the goods they will lose support and hence some of their capacity for self regulation. Hence the pressure on professions to give their own public account of their work.

Duties to the profession. Individual professionals are held to have an obligation to the profession to help fulfil its wider social role. Professionals have a duty to uphold the values of the profession and throughout their work they represent the profession. In this way, for example lawyers are considered to have a professional duty to act in an exemplary law-like manner and even minor illegal acts are treated severely by professional associations. Professionals themselves have an obligation to assist in internal reform because only those in a profession can do this.

5. Philosophy as a profession

> The very concept one has of one's role as a professional tends to shape one's professional ethics. (Callaghan, 1980)

In support of my claim that it makes sense to view philosophy as a profession I offer some, I hope, reasonably uncontroversial observations of the way that philosophy is practised in the West. With regard to philosophy's self-identification or corporate image space allows only a few significant textual examples. Overall I claim that this perspective can give guidelines for constructive thinking about problems of applied philosophy in its relation to philosophy as a whole and hence, derivatively, guidelines for thinking about professional ethics.

Firstly, there is no doubt that a general precondition of practising philosophy in the West is an extensive training through an academic institution. The way in which most philosophers earn their living is by teaching philosophy which is professionalized in a fairly high degree in that access to posts is generally regulated by philosophers. (Of course teaching itself in the academy is not professionalized to any significant degree — a fact perhaps underlined by the lack of attention to the professional ethics of teaching.) In practice there is great pressure not only to be philosophically trained but to also be philosophically employed to be an accepted part of the philosophical community. With regard to the provision of services I argue that philosophy does provide professional services not only to students but also to the wider community — and it is an aspect that I will elaborate in section 6.

To what extent then, is the philosophical community identifiable as a profession? The attacks on philosophy as an academic subject together with closures of departments have resulted in overt attempts to codify the excellences of philosophy and justify its social and economic value. (As in the production of an account for employers of the benefits of a philosophy degree.) The pressure to demonstrate the relevance of philosophy has been a spur to the development of applied philosophy — in common with the adaptation necessary for economic survival. It does seem, however, that it is only under pressure that philosophy has begun to talk to 'outsiders' about what it is. It should also be noted that the changes in philosophy have brought about some professional tensions between applied philosophy and philosophy considered as the study of first principles and classic problems. This is the theme of the presidential address to the Southwestern Philosophical Society by Don Marquis. This is a marvellous document in the sociology of philosophy as the president clearly feels under such pressure to seal the professional boundaries of philosophy that he refers to that 'out-group' 'amateur metaphysicians' as

34

a breed, we might agree, to be avoided at all costs (Marquis, 1990).

A further example of professional identification comes in an introduction to a collection entitled 'Applied Philosophy' by Peter Singer (Singer, 1986). Peter Singer enthusiastically hails the acceptance of the social value of applied ethics by the broader community. He interprets the appointment of Mary Warnock to chair the Committee of Inquiry into Human Fertilisation and Embryology by the British Government as symptomatic of this community acceptance. In addition he cites the enshrinement of philosophers in licensing processes as an example of great public trust in the profession. The word 'profession' itself is very rarely used by philosophers to refer to philosophy — one usage is found in the Society for Applied Philosophy's entrance criteria for the annual essay prize where it is stated that entrants must not be 'professional philosophers'.

I conclude that philosophy is a profession despite the lack of conscious recognition of this fact. Furthermore I argue that the profession of philosophy is currently significantly widening its social mandate for the exercise of professional skills and opinion. If we do accept that professions in positions of power do have a public duty, we must consider more explicitly what the professional duties of philosophy to the wider community might be. Only then will we be able to ensure consistency between those duties and the individual exercise of professional opinion and skills.

6. The professional role of philosophy in the community

I will not attempt to give anything like a complete account of the professional duties of philosophers, confining myself to arguing for the necessary (but not sufficient) professional values of reflection and argumentation (in the sense of demonstration, not contention). I propose that the professional values of any specific section of philosophy should reflect these central values of the wider philosophical enterprise.

The necessity of reflection and argumentation

Philosophy overall asserts the value of reflection, whether reflection on first principles or reflection on the significance of certain kinds of action. I suggest that a philosopher who did not assert the value of reflection would be a contradiction in terms. The second distinctive feature of philosophy is that it attempts to convince by argumentation. Argumentation is a model of structured communication that assumes an argument will be assessed on its merits, without appeals to authority. In this way argumentation is an inherently democratic model of influence, assuming

35

as it does that the correspondent is of equal status (Habermas, 1972).

I would argue that if professionals do have a wider duty to society then part of that duty must be to widen the appreciation, understanding and utilization of the values specific to the profession. This is one reason that we accept that every profession will have significantly different ethical codes. Therefore, at least part of the social mission of philosophy should be to elevate the role of reflection and argumentation into an important part of civil life (Tinder, 1980). This does represent a return to the earliest conception of philosophy, involving, not a claim to ethical expertise, but a commitment to the canons of clear argument and open debate (Almond and Hill, 1991). This duty implies the role of enabling not directing public debate.

Philosophy and advocacy

In this section I distinguish between different senses of 'advocacy' in the professional philosophical context. In one sense 'advocacy' can relate back to the notion of the 'client group' of a profession. Although I have said the major client group of philosophy is students, there is another sense of client that is defined by a relationship of advocacy. Philosophers may choose to take the experiences and interests of a particular group as a starting point for their work, this happens for example in feminist philosophy. This may be advocacy in the following sense, a translator rather than a controller; not dominating the client but translating the client's objectives into the terms of accepted discourse' (Cotterell, 1982). This is the kind of advocacy that allows more voices to contribute to the social democratic conversation. This may step outside of philosophy when it extends to helping certain groups achieve specific political objectives; this may be a matter of concern if a philosopher uses their professional prestige to help to do this.

The professional duty of enabling public debate which I have suggested above does not at all preclude the advocacy of widely differing philosophical positions. However, it does suggest a minimum requirement that public expressions of philosophical advocacy should be accessible to public debate and criticism. The judicious combination of both an enabling function and particular advocacy is in fact an accepted part of professional philosophical life. In teaching, one expects to deliver many different philosophical views and impart the skills to assess these; in publication and one's own work philosophical advocacy is expected. I am, in part, arguing here for a more conscious attention to including both these aspects in regard to relations with the wider community.

Applied philosophy does help engage the wider community in reflective dialogue through the production of relevant (and relatively accessible) argumentation on important social questions. In engaging critically with substantive public issues applied philosophy carries out one important aspect of the professional duties of philosophy as a whole, for which it should receive due support from the rest of the philosophical community. As that part of the professional community which is in closest relation to the public the professional values of philosophy are communicated to the public primarily through these channels. Perhaps this partly accounts for the critical pressure from the rest of the profession.

I would argue that the general philosophical values of reflection and argument partly find expression in the specific area of moral philosophy through the value accorded to moral autonomy. Moral philosophers committed to the importance of moral autonomy cannot consistently uphold a view of the public as needing to be 'trained' in moral values. The focus of moral philosophy is not advocacy of the existing laws of society, but rather in developing and promoting the means of their rational assessment by the community. For example raising public awareness of the ethics of sustainability is not a matter of issuing new sets of ethical prescriptions but of introducing ethical concepts of sustainability into moral discourse (NIACE, 1993). In this way it is ethically necessary for the public to have some part in apprehending and defining the moral content and relevance of situations and technologies (Winner, 1992). It is therefore necessary for the work of applied philosophy to be presented essentially as part of a social dialogue.

7. Models of expertise and constituencies of opinion

Expertise

We have seen that philosophers on expert committees are frequently referred to as 'experts' in ethics. I will argue that the concept of 'expertise' is understood within a model that does not apply to philosophy. This is not necessarily a problem of philosophers' own making except insofar as philosophy fails to communicate its specific nature, not only to the public but to other professions and disciplines. The mistaken recognition of moral philosophers as 'experts' seems endemic in expert committees. Firstly, it is undoubtedly prestigious to be a member of such a committee, and there is an enhancement of professional status. I feel there is no doubt that the substantive judgements of such 'ethical experts' would be given great weight. I argue that this is not a state of affairs that moral philosophers should relish and employ to deliver their own ethical commitments into policy.

I contend that philosophers are in danger of misplaced recognition as experts because of the normative expert paradigm of other professions. For example, law and medicine. In both of these cases the experts stand in relation to a set of accepted texts and opinions. Clearly there is leeway in interpretation, but in both cases the individual 'expert' has an institutional mandate which will form a normative structure for their deliberations. With regard to moral philosophers there is an important structural difference — there is no developed, internally coherent body of moral knowledge to which philosophers have privileged access. There is a relationship to a body of tradition, but the relationship is rather one of 'critically valuing' (Parker, 1993).

Constituencies of opinion

If, as I have argued, philosophers cannot be considered 'experts' in the normative sense, perhaps their role on expert committees is seen rather as representatives of secular ethical opinion, in the same way as religious representatives? It is instructive to compare the two cases. In the case of the religious representative, the expertise is in religious doctrine, which is related to the views and feelings of believers. However, there is no question of the religious representative having a mandate from the believers, church doctrine is not decided by simple majority but by religious experts. The expert representative of a constituency of religious opinion has a normative foundation which, I have argued the philosopher cannot have. It is only this difference which can refute Ayer's critique of moral philosophy as 'lay sermonising' (Ayer, 1936).

Moral Philosophers cannot stand in the same relation as legal and religious experts to their respective constituencies of opinion. Perhaps this has led to a weakening and underestimation of the extent of secular ethical feeling. However, the relationship of 'enabling' moral reflection must be maintained in its difference from that of the expert on secular values. It may be there is a case for specifically including representatives of organizations that espouse certain aspects of the western humanist tradition, but that would not be a specifically philosophical role. It cannot be the case, either, that philosophers have expert knowledge of the actual distribution of opinions on the subject under discussion (however such opinion might be measured). Such an expert on secular values would be a sociologist not a philosopher, though there is clearly a need for some joint work to be done in the sphere of public ethics.

Philosophical expertise

The acceptable sense of philosophical expertise is thus primarily an expertise in enabling debate. This involves analysis, a familiarity with the kinds of questions under discussion and familiarity with a variety of views on those questions. Using these skills the philosopher may help achieve the most extensive possible ethical consensus on a subject — but could still consistently advocate some other set of views as being better.

I suggest that there has been a confusion which has prevented proper attention to the professional contexts of applied philosophy. Applied philosophy has necessarily moved away from that ethical scepticism which only allowed an analytic metaethical role for philosophy. However, to question the validity of concepts of ethical expertise it is not necessary to assume a sceptical position. It is quite possible to hold the objectivity of moral knowledge without claiming that one has privileged access to that knowledge. My argument for exercising care in moral advocacy is not based on scepticism but on a commitment to the philosophical values of open debate.

Conclusion

I conclude that the professional duty of moral philosophers on expert committees is primarily to help build the community of moral inquiry and hence uphold values that are a necessary part of philosophy. This means that we must pay attention to the institutional aspects of committees such as dissemination of information and public participation. If we do not do this we run the risk of our dialogical contributions being used as products and fed into undemocratic processes. Equally, there are professional dangers in expert committee work. One danger mentioned by the European report is lack of independence — this may be easy to identify at an institutional level but similar issues arise when governments seek to annexe the prestige of philosophy. I believe that it would also be helpful to philosophers to open up discussion of professional dilemmas — those situations where the demands of work and the demands of philosophy come into conflict.

There is a need for philosophers to communicate the nature of philosophy both to other professionals and the lay community. It has been proposed that professional codes are one way that professions do communicate their specific nature although there are doubts as to their effectiveness in guiding action (Beyerstein, 1993). Although we are unused to considering philosophy in this light, to have professional power without the limitations of an overt professional status is inimical to the open society to which I have argued philosophy must aspire.

There is clearly an implicit criticism in this paper of expert committees as innately undemocratic in structure. I believe this is to be a particular danger where results feed too directly into legislation with only a superficial public debate. If, as I have argued, philosophical method has aspects that are innately democratic then the possibility that philosophers could contribute to an attenuation of democracy should be of great professional concern. A disabling profession of applied ethics would be one that performs in the wake of new technologies as an institutional part of a process of change, side-steps argumentation and allows a misuse of philosophy's reputation for impartiality. The evidence suggests that this disabling profession could already be developing. I propose that to avoid this we must clearly reference our applied ethics to our philosophical roots, seeing our successes not in the adoption of our own viewpoints, but in the generation of a morally conscious community.

Notes

1. References in this section are to Illich (1977) unless otherwise stated.
2. References in this section are to Warnock (1984).
3. References are to Council of Europe (1990).
4. The account in this section is drawn from Cotterell (1982), Callaghan (1988) and Bayles (1981).

References

Almond B. and Hill D. (eds) (1991), *Applied Philosophy*, Routledge, London.

Ayer A. (1936), *Language Truth and Logic*, Pelican, London.

Bayles M. (1981), *Professional Ethics*, Wadsworth, London.

Beyerstein D. (1993), 'The Functions and Limitations of Professional Codes of Ethics' in Winkler and Coombs (eds), *Applied Ethics*, Blackwell, Oxford.

Callaghan J. (ed) (1988), *Ethical Issues in Professional Life*, Oxford University Press, Oxford.

Cotterell R. (1982), *The Sociology of Law*, Butterworth, London.

Council of Europe (1990), *Europe and Bioethics*, Strasbourg.

Habermas J. (1972), *Knowledge and Human Interests*, Heinemann, London.

Hughes E. (1963), 'Professions' in Callaghan J. (ed) (1988), *Ethical Issues in Professional Life*, Oxford University Press, Oxford.

Illich I. (ed) (1977), *Disabling Professions*, Marion Boyars, London.

Marquis D. (1990), 'The Role of Applied Ethics in Philosophy', in *Southwest Philosophical Review*, Vol. 6, No. 1.

NIACE (1993), *Adult Learning and the Environment*, The National Institute of Adult and Continuing Education, Leicester.

Parker J. (1993), 'The Democratic Dilemma of Values in Policy' presented at Values and the Environment Conference, University of Surrey. to be published in a collection by Wiley. Ed. Y Guerrier.

Singer P. (ed.) (1986), *Applied Ethics*, Oxford University Press, Oxford.

Stuhr J. (1989), 'On Revisioning Philosophy' in *Philosophy Today*, Vol. 33. No. 3.

Tinder G. (1980), 'Community as Inquiry' in *Thinking*, Vol. 7, No. 3.

Warnock M. (1984), *Report of the Inquiry into Human Fertilisation and Embryology*, Her Majesty's Stationery Office, London.

Winner L. (1992), 'Citizen Virtues in a Technological Order' in Winkler and Coombs (eds) *Applied Ethics*, Blackwell, Oxford.

4 Accountability: The obligation to lay oneself open to criticism

Dick Holdsworth

In the present paper I shall try to argue that accountability is best understood in a context which is broad enough to encompass wider areas of human experience than are customarily associated with the concept.

It seems to me futile to deny that such concepts as responsibility, accountability and liability are often used interchangeably by speakers. It also seems futile to attempt to legislate for any one usage of any one term. But what one can perhaps do is to show that there is potentially something interesting about one of the ways in which 'accountability' can be understood, and to explain where the interest lies. The final aim, perhaps, is an economical use of concepts: one which tends to eliminate duplicative referential effort, remembering St Matthew's warning to philosophers and other people that: 'Every idle word that men shall speak, they shall give account thereof in the day of judgement' (Matthew, XI, 45).

Let us begin by recalling the context of the present discussion, which was a conference on applied philosophy. Applied philosophers are interested by the philosophical problems which arise from real-world situations, and in this case their attention focussed on situations which occur in the practice of a profession. Specifically, this was devised as a conference on professional ethics.

Not all the problems which attract the attention of applied philosophers belong to ethics. Many of the situations which interest them involve rival claims to knowledge and the conflict of beliefs. They are better characterized as epistemic than ethical. The importance of that distinction is alluded to in the title of Almond and Hill (eds.), *Applied Philosophy: Morals and Metaphysics in Contemporary Debate* (1991). The distinction between the epistemic and the ethical is more specifically treated in the chapter in that volume by Moros and others on 'Thinking critically in medicine and its ethics: relating applied science and applied ethics', in which the writers claim to discern a detailed parallelism between (a) the evaluation of factual claims, and (b) the analysis of moral decisions (Moros et al., 1991). Without pursuing Moros et al. all the way through their handling of this issue, I should like to put down a marker here to signal an emphasis on epistemological issues before, but not to the exclusion of, ethical ones. This distinction is relevant when we consider the exercise of professions.

A professional is a knowledge based worker in a defined domain. By the exclusive definition of that domain, the professional has knowledge which other people do not have. In other words, the knowledge pool in a society is not homogeneous: it is heterogeneous, and therefore structured. As in all systems, it is the structure which enables work to be done: the work which professionals do. But within the macro-context of the total system, each micro-situation presents a case of knowledge imbalance: the knowledge imbalance exemplified by the pharmacist and the child who trustingly swallows the white tablet, by dentist and patient, by the engineer who has designed the railway signalling system and the traveller who takes her seat in the train.

It is this imbalance of knowledge which supplies the ethical dimension to the situation. This is an interesting case for those who believe in distributive justice, because we do not necessarily want knowledge to be evenly distributed: I mean, we do not necessarily want everyone to have an equal amount of the same knowledge that their counterparts possess. By all means let everyone be equally knowledgeable, but about varied subjects. The reason is that we live better when our lives are supported by a division of labour. In what sense might we live better thus? The answer is in two parts. First, there is the superior range and volume of goods and services which the system supplies to us, if it is functioning well. Second, there is the opportunity it gives us, subject to the same proviso, for developing our own talents and energies.

The division of labour encourages specialization, and to the individual — so the argument would go — specialization is opportunity. If every family had to be responsible for its own shelter and utensils there would be no nurses, doctors and no hospitals. Nobody who felt an urge to develop a talent in the direction of one of the medical professions would be able to do so. Of course, they might be allowed to do so by consent of their peers, but the moment that is permitted to happen the division of labour has been invented.

It comes down to the availability of time. People can become brain surgeons only if they do not have to spend a large proportion of their day ploughing or harvesting. Conversely, the only kind of society in which brain surgeons can exist is one which entrusts ploughing and harvesting to specialists.

But this creates a kind of society in which people do not share a common experience of work. They do not know what working life is like for the other person. In a society based strongly on the division of labour, such as an industrialized society, one cannot know another person's knowledge. In other societies, where Adam Smith was still unknown, one could do that — at least to a greater extent.

The result is that in the complex society, when situations arise in which praise or blame are to be apportioned, people must explain themselves to each other: they must give an account of themselves. If the praise and blame are to be apportioned justly, the account ought to be true, or at least amenable in principle to detached and skilful criticism.

In other words, there is a link between the quality of the account as a factual statement and the quality of the justice to be meted. We are back at the interface between the ethical and the epistemic. It is not simply a matter of telling the truth. All accounts are selective, and the salience of one element of the narrative by comparison with another is frequently a matter for judgement. The more complex the situation, the more complex the account is likely to be, and the further the account giver is likely to be led from a situation where the account can be 'perfect' — say, a straight yes/no answer to a question like 'When you went off shift did you leave the switch to the back-up system in the 'on' position?'

The more (inherently) imperfect the account, the more rigorous the critique must be, and to become more rigorous it must be fuelled with more information. So the requirement for information rises in proportion to the complexity of the situation, or in other words, the growing number of elements of uncertainty which are intrinsic to it.

Abundant sources of uncertainty are to be found at the frontiers of ;ientific knowledge and technological innovation. This paper is being ,vritten from a background of experience in the profession of technology assessment. Technology assessment is highly specialized in the sense that it is a small, though growing profession, but it is also multidisciplinary, especially in the environment in which people like the present writer practise it: the assessment of scientific and technological policy options from any or all of the vantage points which are likely to be salient in political debate. The criteria therefore are not only technical but may also be economic, social or environmental.

At the level of the European Community, technology assessment of one kind or another is conducted by various different units in the European Commission and, at the European Parliament, by the STOA Programme (scientific and technological options assessment). Among the twenty people in the STOA team, at least one person has to take on a managerial role, and this entails a large proportion of administration, and a smaller proportion of research. In between the two comes the task of drawing up research programmes and of defining, in cooperation with the specialist scientific colleagues, both the objectives of assessment projects and the strategies for attaining those objectives. The quest for options is the quest for criteria, and one is continually finding that questions which the inquirer probably supposes to be purely empirical involve difficult problems of conceptualization.

The point of explaining about this work is to show how people trying to provide technology assessment for elected representatives are continually put in the following situation: that of being asked what the inquirer supposes to be first order questions and then discovering that the job of answering them demands, as a prerequisite, the elucidation of a range of second order puzzles.

This is not an introduction to the ethics of technology assessment as a profession, but some background to the issues which confront those who practise it. These issues are of wide ranging scope, which cross national frontiers and the borders of many different professions. Often they emerge into the political arena because an untoward incident has occurred, or because the future occurrence of one is feared. In such circumstances, attention naturally focuses on the actual or putative culprits, and the task of assessment may well become linked, or be seen to be linked to the elaboration of new forms of regulation. In this context, one encounters the problem of deciding what forms of regulation are necessary and fair, including the option of deregulation or the simple absence of regulation.

Let me mention some examples of topics which have, or might have been referred to a parliamentary technology assessment unit at European level. All of these topics have been the subject of European legislation :

Environmental impact assessment
Eco-auditing
The Seveso Directive on the use of dangerous substances
The deliberate release of genetically modified organisms

Before considering these examples more closely, let us pause for a moment on the idea of accountability as something to do with the quest for culprits and the imperatives of retribution, as implied in the following things which people often say:

'I'll hold you accountable for this.'
'You're going to have to account for this to me.'
'I've got an account to settle with you.'

Never a day goes by without the news media reporting a demand that some person or authority be made accountable for one activity or another which has rendered itself problematical. So at first sight accountability seems to be about apportioning blame. But if so, in what way does it differ from responsibility, say, or liability?

There are locutions in which the vocabulary of accountability sounds more positive. Consider these examples:

'She gave a good account of herself.'
'I questioned the senior operator, and his account stands up.'
'The hotel staff have accounted for their movements on the evening of the crime.'

I would argue that what these negative and positive examples show is that the rendering of an account of what has happened when something goes wrong is highly relevant to the issue of who is to get the blame, but it is not the same thing as an ascription of blame. It is a necessary prerequisite for the ascription of responsibility. When we have studied the account of the incident, we shall draw a conclusion of who was responsible for what went wrong, and then — subject to the provisions of law currently in force — that person will probably be held liable by a court for the damage which resulted.

When we have read the account and seen what happened, we may perhaps conclude that the person responsible for the organization or place in which the incident happened was not responsible for the incident itself. In the situation, various levels and types of responsibility will be discernible. These include the responsibility to give an account. It can be a serious fault not to have given an account. Imagine an explosion has occurred at an industrial plant, and a manager is questioning an operator:

'When did you notice the pressure had gone up?'
'At half past one.'
'Did you tell the senior operator?'
'Not right away. I thought the gauge might be faulty.'

The key element, both while the incident is happening and in the aftermath, is the transfer of relevant information. And at any given point along the line, there is always a responsibility to provide an account: the account which may be used as a basis for conclusions about the ascription of blame, or praise.

This distinguishes between the responsibility to provide the account from the responsibility for the incident. It is not a claim that the two responsibilities never coincide. Indeed they often do. But we should not

46

confuse the one with the other. What often causes us to do so is our experience of human nature. We know perfectly well that when the search for culprits is on, veracious accounts are at a premium. We know that the persons with the biggest share of responsibility for the disaster are the ones most likely to give a false account of events, and we feel very strongly that in nailing their lie we are fixing their blame. The two things seem to fuse into one. But in truth they remain distinguishable.

Now let us return to the items of European legislation which I have already mentioned. I should like to look at them in the context of the approach epitomized by a report entitled *Communicating Risks of Industrial Activities* (Netherlands Organisation for Technology Assessment (NOTA), 1991). The English summary begins by referring to the disasters at Seveso in 1976 (a dioxin leak) and Bhopal in 1984 (methyl isocyanate), and states that since they occurred the importance of providing governments and the public with information on industrial hazards has increasingly been recognized. As a result, the subject of risk communication has received much attention in recent years, both in practice and in research. Citing Covello (1986), the report goes on to say that: 'Risk communication can be described as "any purposeful exchange of information about health or environmental risks between interested parties"' (NOTA, 1991, p. 3).

Risk communication, the report suggests, can be organized into four general types, according to the intended effect of the communication:

1. information and education
2. behaviour change and protective action
3. disaster warnings and emergency information
4. joint problem solving and conflict resolution

The report suggests three reasons for growing interest in risk communication:

> First, there is a tendency within society to interpret problems as information problems. Second, it has become clear that planning for emergencies is an important means of reducing the negative effects of a disaster. And third, risk communication can be used to strengthen confidence in corporate safety policies or to restore it when accidents have occurred (NOTA, 1991, p. 4).

I intend to argue that this list, though accurate as far as it goes, misses out one motive for promoting risk communication which is of especial importance, although I acknowledge that the motive I am going to talk about is foreshadowed in the first of the above points, the fact that there

47

is a tendency within society to interpret problems as information problems. I now propose to examine this informational aspect, and to do this through the four examples of European Community legislation which have already been mentioned.

Environmental impact assessment (EIA) is the subject of an EC Directive (27 June 1985). To quote a summary by the Department of Trade and Industry:

> The Directive requires that for certain types of development which are likely to have significant environmental effects, the appropriate consent shall not be given without those effects being considered. The type of developments which are or may be subject to environmental assessments are listed in Annexes to the Directive, and include steel works, integrated chemical installations, oil refineries,waste disposal plants, aerodromes, holiday villages, industrial estates, paper mills etc. For projects which require environmental assessment, developers are required to provide environmental statements which will describe the projects, their potential environmental effects, and measures which will be taken to avoid or reduce any significant adverse effects (DTI, 1992).

The EIA Directive is of course only one item in a panoply of safety reporting obligations laid by European national or Community legislation on undertakings using potentially hazardous substances.

A recent STOA project paper entitled *Industrial Hazards: the Seveso Directive* (Reyneri, 1993) notes that, at national level, measures for risk assessment go back to the 19th century. France is said to have drawn up its first classification of hazardous establishments in 1870. Turning to more recent developments at European Community level, the paper prints a table listing fifteen proposals for EC legislation or other action in this area being promoted in the 1990s (Reyneri, 1993, p. 6). Many of these have a strong information component, in that they lay down rules for classification, assessment principles and data bank management. (There are also Community R&D activities in the area, not included in that list). The paper goes on to consider, specifically, the issue of updating the Seveso Directive. This is Directive 82/501/EEC which was introduced in 1982 in reaction to the Seveso disaster, and is a Directive 'on the major accident hazards of certain industrial activities'.

Considering, first, the application of the original Seveso Directive, the paper reflects that the information at present available on the current state of implementation in each Member State is 'limited' and says:

This is mainly due to the fact that the original powers granted to the Commission ... were not sufficient to require the information needed to effectively maintain the practical implementation of the Directive.

The information ... has been voluntarily provided by Member States in response to questionnaires ... (Reyneri, 1993, p. 10).

Nevertheless, the Directive does require certain information rules. There is an obligation to inform members of the public about safety measures in the event of an emergency. There is an obligation on plant operators to produce safety reports and submit them for assessment to the competent authority at national or regional level. (An interesting analysis of the public information requirements of the Seveso Directive has been made for the Commission by a team led by Brian Wynne of the University of Lancaster. They found, inter alia, that an information exercise alone is not effective unless accompanied by related social initiatives which assist in developing community relations constructively.) (Wynne, 1992).

This safety report — distinct from the accident report — receives new emphasis in the Commission's proposal for updating the precautions in the Seveso Directive. The safety report will have to include a new section on management systems and organization of the establishment.

The situation concerning the Seveso Directive has been described at some length to estimate the role of information and reporting requirements in legislation currently in force or contemplated.

There are two other areas where information instruments are also important, and which I should like to mention. One is the European Commission's proposal for a voluntary Community eco-audit scheme. (The UK already has a voluntary instrument in this area: the British Standards Institution's standard BS 7750, which defines a number of potential environmental management systems which companies can choose to adopt.)

The European scheme, as proposed, would consist of the following activities:

1. An initial review by the company (or external contractors) of the site concerned showing actual and potential problems caused by the activities on the site.

2. Then, on the basis of the above, production of an environmental protection system consisting of an explicit policy statement, an implementation programme and a management system defining responsibility and tasks.

3. Following the audit itself, the company will release a company environmental statement aimed at the general public outlining performance, objectives, etc.

4. Validation of the audit by an accredited auditor and periodic updates.

The authors of a recent STOA report on the proposed scheme (Imrie and Reyneri, 1993) commend the scheme for the coverage of topics which is envisaged in the eco-audit. This would go beyond simple emissions to, for example, the management of energy, raw materials and waste, and external information and public participation. Points of criticism include the fact that it is voluntary, and the list of exemptions from the scheme (such as public sector undertakings).

My fourth example is Directive 90/220/EEC of 23 April 1990 on 'The deliberate release to the environment of genetically modified organisms' As analysed by the DTI, this Directive aims to control both the release of genetically modified organisms into the environment for research and development and the placing on the market of products containing or consisting of genetically modified organisms. It requires that releases are subject to full review and take place only after a full assessment of both human and environmental safety and the granting of a consent by the competent authority. The DTI says (DTI, 1994) the Directive has been implemented in Great Britain by *The Genetically Modified Organisms (Deliberate Release) Regulations* (1992), which were due to come into force on 1 February 1993, and Part VI of the Environmental Protection Act 1990, as well as certain 1992 Regulations made under section 156 of the Environmental Protection Act 1990 (Statutory Instrument 1992, no. 2617).

Under this Directive a key role is played by the 'notification' which must be submitted by any organization contemplating the release of GMOs into the environment or their placing on the market. There are rules for the format of the notification and for the format of the summary of the notification. The notification is analysed by authorities in the Member State, and, after assessment of any risk, the release is endorsed or refused.

The Commission also receives the information contained in the notifications and maintains an information exchange service vis-à-vis the Member States. While not publishing commercially confidential information thus exchanged among the authorities involved, the Commission does have to publish, in the Official Journal, a list of all products finally endorsed. There is also a requirement for adequate information to be provided to local inhabitants before a deliberate release of GMOs.

The GMOs Directive has been portrayed (Fait, 1992) as epitomizing a shift in approaches to environmental protection from the last minute reaction to a near disaster situation (as when the use of organochlorine insecticides by British farmers threatened the extinction, says Fait, of peregrine falcons, golden eagles and sparrow-hawks) towards a precautionary, just in case strategy. Fait says that meanwhile opinion has shifted in some sectors of the industry — though not all — against the precautionary principle because of the high cost to companies of uncertainty and delay over regulatory decisions.

I should like to pick on a different aspect of the legislative instruments which have been discussed here and that is the extent to which (a) they enshrine the idea that industrial actors must provide accounts of the activities as part of the satisfaction of their obligation to society, and (b) that, albeit slowly, the requirements for accountability are showing signs of widening in scope in the direction of an information flow which will or would involve all three acknowledged phases of an activity: before, during and after.

From this point of view the 'precautionary' quality of legislation which demands an environmental impact assessment before a plant is constructed, a safety report before the plant may use hazardous substances, a notification before genetically modified organisms are used in the contained environment of an R&D or production facility, and another notification before GMOs may be released into the environment is not the salient feature of the new trend. The salient thing is not that we are moving our attention from 'after' the accident has happened to 'before' the accident which we hope will not happen, it is that we are — it seems — filling in the chronological gaps, so that there is continuous attention, before, during and after.

This represents a conception of accountability as chronologically continuous. It is consistent with my view that 'accountability' cannot and should not be reserved for the ex post ascription of blame.

If there is any chance that our activities, though in themselves innocent and benign, involve risk of accident, it may not be unreasonable to make us account for our planning and conduct of the activities: to place us under an obligation to provide such accounts — to make us accountable.

Earlier I made the point that abundant sources of uncertainty are to be found at the frontiers of scientific knowledge and technological innovation. This is indeed the case. I also referred to the complexity of modern industrialized societies and the fact that they are based on an intricate division of labour. I said the essence of the division of labour was the employment of time: that people do not, as a rule, have time to be both a brain surgeon and a farmer. I shall now try to draw these spreads together.

A professional I defined as 'a knowledge based worker in a defined domain'. I am aware that there are alternative, sociological definitions, but here I am deliberately setting the activities of the profession in the context of an analysis of society as a community of knowledge. More specifically, this community is to be recognized by its dynamic. The community of knowledge is not a static repository of knowledge: it is a system for acquiring knowledge. It has to be, because of the phenomenon of experience. Our experience of a changing environment, especially in a changing social environment, involves us whether we intend it or not in the knowledge of new things. Many of those new things demand an adaptation on our part. We try out strategies of adaptation, and we find out which ones work and which ones do not work. At the most immediate, practical level, this knowledge comes to us unbidden. But in a complex society, there are remote sources of influence on our lives which are not themselves immanent in our experience. Channels for the communication of information between them and us have to be deliberately created. That they should account to us, and we to them, will not necessarily just happen. For it to occur, there must be mutual recognition of an obligation to provide accounts.

The portrayal here of society as a community of human beings striving to adapt to a changing environment by testing alternative hypotheses of survival deliberately aligns itself with Popper's evolutionary epistemology, part of which — in *Objective Knowledge* — is the idea that, from the amoeba to Einstein, the acquisition of knowledge always proceeds in the same way: by trial and error (Popper, 1972).

This is correctly seen as an evolutionary perspective, because it sets the acquisition of knowledge in an environment characterized by uncertainty. Some people rebel at the theory of evolution — and analogies derived from it — because they think of natural selection as a stern enforcer of orthodoxy. This is a misunderstanding. In fact what the theory of evolution teaches us is that there are no universal criteria of fitness: the genetic orthodoxy presenting at this instant of time is contingent on a configuration of environmental conditions which may change in the next moment — which may indeed have changed a moment ago, though we have not noticed it yet. In human society, changes in the individual's environment are changes in the knowledge situation of her contemporaries. When your colleagues and neighbours learn new things they start acting in new ways, and you have to adjust to that. At that stage, the emphasis has shifted from 'objective knowledge' to 'the poverty of historicism' — the argument that we cannot foretell the future because our future depends on what we and other people are going to know at the given future point in time, and since those things are by definition not known we cannot know their effects (Popper, 1975).

My argument is that the uncertainty we confront when dealing with science and technology is not just a data deficit, but something intrinsic to the dynamic knowledge community in which we have our social being.

In a dynamic community of knowledge there are periodic stocktakings of the world about us, which often result in a shock, because we then learn that changes have been going on of which we were unaware.

Such a shock was provided by Rachel Carson's book, *Silent Spring* (1962), on the effect of pollution caused by human agency on natural systems in the physical environment. The main object of concern in the book was the impact of modern chemicals such as insecticides. As everyone knows, the book had a revolutionary effect on many people's thinking, making them much more aware of this type of problem.

Having registered that, let us now turn to a paper by Dietrich Henschler (1993) of the University of Wurzburg on 'Environment and human health'. This paper presents a graph of the number of known chemical compounds as registered in the *Chemical Abstracts*. The starting date is 1950, when the figure was about 1 million. In the early years thereafter, the slope of the curve is still quite flat, but from about 1970 it begins to rise steeply until by 1988 the number has reached about 9 million — i.e., something like eight or nine times the number in 1962 when *Silent Spring* was published.

This is not to assert anything negative or positive about the products created by the chemical industry in recent decades. Henschler points out that chemistry is a science and as such lives from innovation and from the invention of marketing of new compounds. The point I wish to make here simply concerns the extreme difficulty — if not the impossibility — of us as citizens directly and comprehensively monitoring the emergence of every new knowledge product as it appears. We have not got, we could not have the time.

When people first read *Silent Spring*, they suddenly became aware that they had failed to take note of a process of change in their environment which had been going on steadily for years and had resulted in an appreciable impact. But that stocktaking was not a definitive redressing of the balance of knowledge. On the contrary, lay people may well now be less well placed to keep track of what is happening in this sector than they were in 1962. Indeed, this must be so.

How then can industry, and science and technology, be made accountable to society? In so far as they answer to the institutions of the state, which are — hypothetically — in the hands of elected representatives, how can MPs account to the electorate for the discharge of their responsibilities?

A provisional answer is: by improving the quality of the information process — not simply giving the lay public a subject of technical information which we do not have time to digest — but by providing the prerequisite for a rigorous critique of planned or accomplished technical activities. That prerequisite is an account. The account may be prospectively oriented, like an environmental impact assessment, or retrospectively, like

53

an accident report under the Seveso Directive. Either way the account supplies the raw material for the trial and error process of knowledge growth.

Take an example of retrospective account giving, arising from the Bhopal accident in 1984. H.W. Lewis, the author of *Technological Risk* (1990), has written as follows:

> One of the imperatives of the risk business is to learn from experience. As Santayama said, 'Those who cannot remember the past are condemned to repeat it'...
> So we may ask: who (in the United States) had the responsibility to learn the lessons of the Bhopal accident? It was, after all, the most lethal industrial accident in history, and there must be important lessons here, after the finger-pointing ends. Soon after the accident this author phoned a friend in a high position in the White House, to ask just which government agency had the responsibility to collect the Bhopal lessons, especially those that cross institutional lines. His response was, 'That's a very interesting question, I guess nobody.' And that's the way it stands today, which is why we appoint a new presidential commission every time there is a new disaster. That we need to learn from experience is a real lesson, waiting patiently to be learned from experience (Lewis, 1990, p. 133).

That much of science lives from innovation is a reminder of something else: that scientific research creates opportunities for people to express their creativity, using in the process skills and knowledge they have built up over years of study and training, which have usually demanded a substantial investment of public money. Outlets for trained talent are a precious resource in the kind of society that is ours. The professions, whether based on natural science or other types of knowledge, are playing a double role: they are providing services, and they are providing opportunities to serve, to those people who have — one way or another — acquired the strong desire to seek out such opportunities. The fact that, from self-interest, some people will abuse the opportunities they secure only makes those chances which remain more valuable.

This sketch of the almost inconceivably rapid transformations at work in our knowledge environment has left those anguished individuals, the citizens of the knowledge community, shrouded in a mist of uncertainty. A possible way out was indicated: a mutual pact to submit accounts of their own activities to the security of the collectivity. The Popperian mist of uncertainty, in these circumstances, perhaps becomes a Rawlsian blindness (Rawls, 1972). Then none of them know from which source the greatest risk comes: from their own activities or those of others. They must pledge themselves to give the fullest and most open account of their works, in order to secure reciprocity from others who otherwise, either subject them to high and secret risks, or, exact large penalties from themselves if it is their own activities which cause disaster.

The social contract scenario certainly seems to be set. One alternative — the utility calculus — is hardly a ready instrument. How does one evolve a regulation of industrial activities based on utilitarian principles in a situation characterized by uncertainty? What is the meeting place of the utilitarian calculus and risk analysis? Answers may be offered to this question, but to deal with the risk analysis of causal effects characterized by nonlinear relationships (such as the effect of carcinogens), they will have to be very sophisticated ones.

In his book *Earth in the Balance*, Al Gore frequently uses the metaphor of the 'Faustian pact' (Gore, 1992). He means that we have struck a deal with the devil in accepting short term gains in economic growth at the price of the massive long term costs of environmental degradation.

Is the Rawlsian pact any better than the Faustian one, if it allows risks to continue to be incurred? In order to answer 'yes' it would be necessary to make the following argument:

1. The Rawlsian pact is to accept that activities involving some measure of risk will continue, provided that the risk is low.

2. The trade-off is between a licence to operate and an obligation to provide accounts of operations, open to criticism.

3. In making the pact, we risk little since an optimized information flow will be a great improvement on what we had before, and it will make it easier for us to identify and eliminate high risk activities.

4. The 'licence to operate' for industry provides an outlet for the creativity of trained talent: it implies a licence to exercise a profession, though the two things are not identical.

5. Thus we could emerge from a state of nature, characterized by iterative zero-sum battles over arbitrarily selected regulatory disputes, to a situation which Rousseau himself might have approved, in which all the citizens of the knowledge community cede unreservedly all their knowledge to the community and receive in return the right to apply it.

The citizens sit enshrouded in a logically necessary fog of evolutionary uncertainty so impenetrable that it conceals from them their own nature and their own interest. As Rawls put it, 'The principles of justice are chosen behind a veil of ignorance.' Do the citizens now seal the Rawlsian pact — yes, or no? The verdict is yours.

References

Almond, Brenda and Hill, Donald (eds.), (1991), *Applied Philosophy: Morals and Metaphysics in Contemporary Debate*, Routledge, London.

Carson, Rachel (1962), *Silent Spring*, Houghton Mifflin, Boston.Department of Trade and Industry (1992) Spearhead database, 6 November.

Department of Trade and Industry (1994), Spearhead database, 14 January.

EC (1985) Directive 85/337/EEC, 27 June.

Fait, Joyce (1992), 'Who's afraid of biotechnology?', *New Scientist*, vol. 134, no. 1827.

Gore, Al (1992), *Earth in the Balance*, Houghton Mifflin, Boston.

Henschler, Dietrich (1993), *Environment and Health*, STOA, Directorate-General for Research, European Parliament, Luxembourg.

Imrie, Steve and Reyneri, Guido (1993), *Environmental Auditing and the Proposed Eco-audit Scheme*, STOA, Directorate-General for Research, European Parliament, Luxembourg, pp. 8-9.

Lewis, H.W. (1990), *Technological risk*, W.W. Norton, New York.

Matthew, XI, 45.

Moros, Daniel A., Rhodes, R, Baumrin, B., and Strain, James. J. (1991), 'Thinking critically in medicine and its ethics: relating applied science and applied ethics' in Almond, Brenda and Hill, Donald (eds) (1991).

Popper, Karl (1972), *Objective Knowledge — An evolutionary approach*, Oxford University Press, Oxford.

Popper, Karl (1957), *The Poverty of Historicism.*

Rawls, John (1972), *A Theory of Justice*, Oxford University Press, Oxford.

Reyneri, Guido (1993), *Industrial hazards: the Seveso Directive*, STOA, Directorate-General for Research, European Parliament, Luxembourg.

Statutory Instrument (SI) 1992 No. 2617.

Van Eijndhoven, J. and Worrel, C. (eds.), (1991), *Communicating Risks of Industrial Activities*, NOTA (Netherlands Organisation for Technology Assessment), The Hague, The Netherlands.

Wynne, B. (1992), *Empirical Evaluation of Public Information on Major Industrial Accident Hazards*, Institute for Systems Engineering and Informatics, Community Documentation Centre on Industrial Risk, Joint Research Centre, CEC.

5 Accountability and lawyers

Richard H. S. Tur

... with a wig on his head and a band round his neck [a lawyer will]
do for a guinea what without those appendages he would think it
infamous to do for an empire (Macaulay, 1914).

Clients objectives and lawyers responsibilities

Consider the following case (*Spaulding v Zimmerman*, 1962)[1]: a motorist
negligently collides with and injures a pedestrian. Both parties consult
lawyers. Both lawyers obtain medical reports. The medical report obtained
by the motorist's lawyer indicates an aorta aneurism, caused by the
collision, which is life-threatening though safely operable whereas the
medical report obtained by the pedestrian's lawyer makes no mention of
any such condition. In the course of negotiations it soon becomes
apparent to the motorist's lawyer that the pedestrian's lawyer is wholly
unaware of the existence of the aorta aneurism and is willing to accept on
behalf of the injured client a sum considerably lower than appropriate to
the actual circumstances. In that state of knowledge, does the motorists
lawyer do anything improper in concluding a binding settlement at the
lower figure? Is it ethical for a lawyer to take advantage of the other sides
ignorance of crucial facts?

On the standard conception of the lawyers role (Luban, 1988), the
motorist's lawyer has no professional ethical duty to disclose to the other
side, or to anyone else, the existence of the aorta aneurism. Indeed, on
that same standard conception, the motorist's lawyer has a duty not to
disclose any such information. The standard conception is that the lawyer
is not accountable for the consequences of zealous and single-minded
pursuit of·the interests of the client.

In its extreme form the standard conception invokes the image of the lawyer as 'hired gun'.[2] On such an instrumentalist conception, a 'good lawyer' is simply one who is effective in facilitating or realizing objectives externally determined by clients, irrespective of the moral quality of these objectives. A particularly 'good lawyer', on this instrumentalist view, is one who makes the law serve the interests of clients, even to the extent of reconstructing the law, taking advantage of loopholes in the law, subverting the (presumed) intentions of the legislature, and thwarting its (presumed) objectives where necessary in order to deliver.

On this view of lawyering, sophisticated and subtle restructuring of clients finances in order to minimize liability to taxation or to child maintenance is wholly legitimate. Indeed such conduct may justifiably be perceived as obligatory upon any lawyer who takes seriously the implications of the professional duty of conscientious and committed pursuit of the clients interests. Whether or not 'law', itself, is an essentially contested concept, legal practice is an adversarial activity and outcomes are frequently contested, sometimes bitterly. Those who object to the outcomes achieved for clients by shrewd tax lawyers and ingenious family practitioners and who therefore charge such practitioners with immorality may fairly be charged themselves with moral insensitivity and a failure to understand the real moral dilemma that faces a conscientious lawyer whose professional duty it is to pursue objectives widely perceived as immoral and, perhaps, also perceived as immoral by the lawyer.

Be all that as it may, on the standard conception lawyers are not morally accountable for the results of their efforts and cannot be made accountable without destroying their essential function. Lawyering thus appears to involve an institutional exemption from the normal dictates of moral conscience. This disturbing conclusion may be reinforced by reference to some of the tacit major premises of lawyering in Anglo-American common law systems.

First, it is for the parties and not for the court to ingather and present both the relevant facts and the applicable law. Such so-called 'party-control' of litigation, however, may, on analysis, prove to be neither economically efficient nor ethically optimal in terms of institutional design in that it may add unnecessarily to costs and provide opportunities and temptations to manipulate procedure in order to foster a favoured outcome, including forum shopping, selective use of expert testimony, and jury vetting.

A second premise is that truth will necessarily emerge out of this clash of zealous advocacy especially if conducted under the watchful eye of an impartial umpire. This institutional application of John Stuart Mill's argument for freedom of expression is, however, here rendered implausible by inequalities of knowledge and access to relevant information, and by judicial commitment to some set of values which may impact adversely upon the clients objectives. In addition, the vast majority of disputes are settled, albeit sometimes 'at the door of the court'. Accordingly, in most disputes the reality is that there is no neutral umpire seeking to ensure fair play in the conduct of the disputants. The parties and their legal advisers determine for themselves just how they will conduct the dispute and some will play hard ball.

A third underlying assumption is that that society is best which facilitates the pursuit by individuals of their own private determined vision of the good. Even if private vice does not lead to public virtue, lawyers should not seek to pass clients ends through any moral filter but should seek only to realise clients' ends, however morally disreputable these may appear to be. Indeed, on liberal assumptions lawyers should not exploit the lawyer-client relationship surreptitiously to enforce their own or community morals. The enforcement of morals is, on this view, no more the business of lawyers than it is on classical liberal arguments any business of the law.

Returning to the case of the injured pedestrian ignorant of the extent and nature of injuries suffered, the standard conception of the lawyers role and established principles of legal ethics lead to an outcome different from that flowing from any critical or positive morality which puts a premium on human welfare. Many people, including some lawyers, have moral difficulty with the case and not only with the 'unfair' outcome in terms of the compensation negotiated which is well short of what is appropriate in all the circumstances of the case but also with the very real risk of an avoidable death flowing from the professional duty of silence.

Clearly, professional ethics fail to be distinguished from both current community standards and critical moralities. So much so that to some philosophers it may appear to be an unacceptable dilution of the concept of 'ethics' to apply that (honorific) term to the practices and standards of working professions, no matter how worthy, internally coherent, well articulated (for example in written codes), and institutionally supported (for example by complaints officers and disciplinary committees). As against which, it is at least for debate whether ethics necessarily entails universalizability or rationality and whether 'role morality' is a legitimate category of ethical discourse. Whatever view one takes of these conceptual questions, the practical question remains: What, if anything, justifies the lawyers institutional exemption from the promptings of moral conscience?

An ethically sensitive lawyer might deny that the lawyers role necessarily involves exemption from moral conscience and seek to regulate the lawyer-client relationship either according to current morality or to principles warranted by one or another critical morality or according to the lawyers own internalized, personal morality. Thus in the case of the

60

pedestrian ignorant of the aneurism such a lawyer would put to the motorist client (or to the insurance company that stands in the motorists shoes) the 'obvious' immorality of taking economic advantage of the pedestrians ignorance and of risking the pedestrians life through nondisclosure. Perhaps such a lawyer would go further and insist, even on pain of withdrawing from the case, on disclosing the existence of the aneurism. Such ethically sensitive conduct, though urged upon lawyers by some, may achieve little and greatly embarrass the lawyer professionally.

If in spite of the 'obvious' immorality the motorist/insurer client insists that the existence of the aneurism be not disclosed, the ethically sensitive lawyer's withdrawal from the case leaves the client free to employ another (possibly less morally sensitive) lawyer and free, too, not to tell the new lawyer anything about the medical report. In such circumstances, the 'obvious' immorality remains. Suppose that the original lawyer therefore goes further and personally discloses directly to the other side the existence of the aneurism. On the standard conception of the lawyers role this is seriously unprofessional in that it breaches the lawyers duties to the client of loyalty and confidentiality and it would also give rise to a cause of legal action sounding in contract for breach, whether or not the client actually chose to institute any such proceedings. Those who advocate greater moral sensitivity and activism in the solicitor-client relationship appear to be more than a tad unrealistic unless the proposal is also radically to revise the adversarial system of justice and the liberal tradition that sustains it. Of course, the adversarial system of justice and the liberal tradition are not immune from criticism and radical revision but if that is the proposal the argument has too swiftly moved a long way from the original focus on professional ethics and accountability and conscientious lawyers can legitimately be heard to ask about their ethical responsibilities here and now, pending radical restructuring, if any, of the adversarial system and liberal society.

Accountability, moral philosophy and applied ethics

For philosophers questions of accountability, including the accountability of professions in general and lawyers in particular, lead very naturally into a discussion of ethical issues and some philosophers are then very quick to privilege their (allegedly universal) concepts and values and impose these upon members of the profession from the outside with little or no appreciation of or respect for the internal structure, including the ethical structuring, of the profession. This rather obviously loads the judgemental dice against the conduct of members of the profession concerned.

For example, from some feminist perspectives a lawyer who defends one charged with rape on the basis of an honest but mistaken belief in consent is simply acting immorally and any reference to the ethics of the lawyers profession is from such a privileged perspective taken only as compounding the original immorality. Again, from a utilitarian perspective a lawyer who, knowing or very strongly believing in a clients guilt, nonetheless puts the prosecution to the time, trouble and substantial expense of proof is to be condemned and the utilitarian will give short shrift to the lawyers own defence that so long as there is a presumption of innocence it is wholly ethical to put the prosecution to proof of its case.

It really is curiously self-defeating and intellectually sterile to consider the ethical quality of the conduct of lawyers only on the hypothesis that lawyers are no different from moral agents in general and to conclude, therefore, that lawyering is necessarily immoral because the lawyers conduct does not conform to the general standards of this or another privileged theory. I take it that at least part of the point of applied philosophy is seriously to reassess general and abstract philosophical theories from the (presumptively valid) perspective of practical activities that appear to be distorted and devalued by the general theory. For example, the general theory of utilitarianism distorts and devalues due process of law. Thus plea-bargaining, despite the known risks of innocents pleading to a lesser charge rather than risk conviction of a greater, is presented as legitimate, perhaps even a required, option from a utilitarian perspective. Anyone who regards innocence as a moral value must have serious reservations not only about plea-bargaining but about any criminal justice system implemented on strict utilitarian lines.

Rather than look at lawyering from the perspective of unmodified utilitarianism and pronounce it ethically defective, I propose as an applied philosopher to look at utilitarianism from the vantage point of lawyering. Among the values embedded in and realised through lawyering (albeit imperfectly in an imperfect world) is the transcendent value of innocence and, indeed, non-degraded Anglo-American lawyering might fairly be regarded as an activity which treats innocence as a non-negotiable value. On that basis plea-bargaining is professionally unethical because it necessarily treats innocence as a negotiable commodity. It treats an accused as means only and not as an end and should be condemned as a perversion and distortion of the criminal justice system.

From an internal perspective conduct that would otherwise justly be criticised as unethical and contrary to the principle of utility, may be seen as ethical, perhaps even heroic. For example, lawyers who acted for those originally convicted of IRA bombing and killings and lawyers who acted in the subsequent successful appeals many years later, despite great unpopularity and hostility, even from fellow lawyers,[3] acted for justice and truth, and refused to treat the innocent victims as means only irrespective of the embarrassment thereby generated for the police forces involved, for the criminal justice system and for the government. It was simply not a moral option for these lawyers to walk away from those asserting their innocence and the heroic quality of the lawyers conduct in these cases would remain even had their side of the argument not ultimately prevailed.

I suggest that ethical assessment of professional conduct ought to take account of the guiding values of the profession and not consist merely of judgement by reference to external (and allegedly universal) ethical principles. I should add that even on an internal assessment, judging lawyers according to standards intrinsic to lawyering, the legal professions in Anglo-American jurisdictions have no cause whatsoever for complacency.[4] For example, at least some of the miscarriages of justice that have disfigured the English criminal justice system recently occurred because some lawyers did not conduct themselves according to the internal values of lawyering. The extent to which lawyers conduct actually falls short of these values is primarily a sociological inquiry whereas the nature and extent of lawyers ethics is a question of applied philosophy.

Legal accountability of lawyers

For lawyers, themselves, and their governing bodies, talk of 'accountability' does not immediately raise questions about lawyers moral responsibility, if any, for clients' objectives. Rather, it raises questions about accountability to clients and to professional bodies for the quality, price and integrity of lawyering, and the conformity of their conduct with the established ethical standards of the community of lawyers to which they belong.

It is helpful conceptually to distinguish inadequate legal services from professional misconduct (*Council of the Law Society of Scotland v J*, 1991), although the distinction is sometimes blurred in practice and in any event clients may be more concerned to obtain a remedy for poor service than to see lawyers disciplined for misconduct. In principle, inadequate legal services will give rise to a cause of action in the courts for breach of contract in that it is an implied term of the retainer that the lawyer has and will exercise appropriate skill and competence.[5] However, a client dissatisfied with a lawyers services, particularly in the conduct of litigation, is unlikely to be enthusiastic about employing another lawyer in order to sue the first or to attempt to conduct such legal action personally. Accordingly there has been a move in recent times statutorily to empower law societies and/or legal services ombudsmen to remit fees and award compensation. It follows that lawyers may be accountable for inadequate legal services, either through the courts or through their professional bodies. It is difficult yet to assess whether these novel procedures will generate and support regimes of adequate compensation or will only operate cheaply to buy off victims of inadequate professional services and minor departures from the ethical standards of the legal professions.

In passing, it should be noted that in common law jurisdictions whether or not legal practitioners are formally divided into two separate and distinctive functional groups as, for example, barristers and solicitors in England, common law grants an immunity, purportedly justified as a matter of public policy, for 'in-court' work. In England barristers enjoy this immunity but given that counsel's opinion will not relieve a solicitor of liability (*Davy-Chiesman v Davy-Chiesman*, 1984, Fam 48) a client with a cause of action may in some circumstances be able to recover from the solicitor despite the barristers immunity. It has seemed to some, including the Law Reform Commission of Victoria (1991), appropriate to question the immunity of advocates from liability for negligent in-court work. The issue is well put by an Australian judge:

> ... the law ought not readily grant privileges or immunities. Favouritism and inequality of treatment under the law are capable of breeding contempt for the law, particularly when it is perceived that those favoured are themselves lawyers ... there is a heavy burden of justification on those who claim an immunity or privilege (*Giannarelli v Wraith*, 1988, 165 CLR 543, 575-6, per Wilson J).

One concern is that if legally liable, in-court lawyers would err on the side of caution and adopt self-protective measures such as calling more witnesses, asking more questions and so forth. In general, exposure to legal liability would compromise the independent judgement of the in-court lawyer. Accordingly, trials would be longer, costs higher, delays greater. If the legal liability of in-court lawyers would impact so adversely on the administration of justice then the immunity could be justified in the public interest even though this leaves losses caused by grossly incompetent in-court lawyering where they fall, that is on the hapless victim, client of the legally unaccountable in-court lawyer. The heavy burden thus cold-bloodedly imposed on innocent victims of in-court lawyer negligence in the name of the efficient administration of justice is no less a case of unfair victimization than is the 'punishment' of an innocent for the good of society at large. In any event, since the argument for the immunity is based on what might happen if the immunity was removed there is little evidence and much speculation. Experience in Ontario, as reported in 1979 (*Demarco v Ungaro*, 1979, 95 DLR (3d) 385) where in-court lawyers have been liable for negligence since 1863 is that actions against lawyers 'had not attained serious proportions'. It is a poor reflection on in-court lawyers that their defenders anticipate a flood of actions for negligence should the immunity be removed. If that apprehension is well founded, there are larger numbers of innocent victims than the critics and reformers suppose caught up in litigation and deprived '...of all redress under the common law for 'in-court' negligence, however gross and callous in its nature or devastating in its consequences' (*Giannarelli v Wraith*, 1988, 165 CLR 543, 588, per Deane J).

Professional accountability and lawyers

Independently of liability in the courts for breach of contract, or for the tort of negligence, where applicable, lawyers are answerable to their professional bodies for their conduct. In some instances it has appeared to professional bodies and regulators that a lawyer is open to investigation and discipline in respect of private and personal conduct no less than in respect of strictly professional activities, at least if that conduct appears likely to bring the legal profession into disrepute. Thus in Scotland a solicitor was disciplined for arranging to obtain a gun from an underworld contact even though the solicitor perhaps had some reason to fear an attack, and the whole matter was conducted away from the solicitor's place of business and outside office hours. In contrast it was not thought appropriate to investigate newspaper allegations that another solicitor had arranged, for payment, sadomasochistic services from a prostitute, or to criticize the solicitor even though such conduct is only distinguishable in degree from that stigmatized as criminal by the House of Lords.[6] Again it appeared to the responsible body that a solicitor acting as a trustee was not subject to professional discipline for conduct as a trustee, even though the conduct in that capacity was open to legitimate criticism and might reasonably be thought to cast an unflattering light on the solicitors profession in Scotland. There would appear to be some confusion in Scotland as to whether or not lawyers ethics apply to lawyers twenty-four hours a day.

In England, the Solicitors Complaints Bureau appeared more confident, responding to a complaint, that whereas it is certainly unprofessional conduct for a solicitor to write offensive or threatening letters when acting as a solicitor, a solicitor who writes such a letter in a 'private' capacity did not fall to be investigated or disciplined. Since the letter in this case was written in connection with a dispute in which a relative was involved with a third party, threatening legal action against the third party on behalf of the relative, and since the solicitor duly appeared in court for the relative in the ensuing litigation, the Solicitors Complaints Bureau appears to have been overly sympathetic to the solicitor involved by taking an unduly wide view of what constitutes private conduct but the underlying assumption was that private conduct, however odious, did not fall within the jurisdiction of the Solicitors Complaints Bureau.

Consideration of such cases suggest that there are at least two problems with self-regulation by the legal professions. First, there is a problem of definition: just what ethical duties are incumbent upon a lawyer by virtue of membership of the legal profession and just when do these duties apply? Secondly there is a problem of natural justice. Basic principles of fairness require that none be judge in their own cause. Put to any lawyer the proposition that there is nothing amiss with police investigating complaints of police corruption or misconduct. Lawyers, especially those with experience of criminal practice, can readily construct an impressive series of arguments for some degree of external or independent review,[7] yet lawyers own organizations defend self-regulation with a tenacity and determination which, together with the obvious special pleading involved, suggests that they might be driven by self-interest.

This is not to say that lawyers organizations cannot adequately review and maintain the ethical quality of members conduct. Some such bodies, including the Law Society of Queensland, proactively offer impressive continuing legal education programmes and treat both educational and disciplinary aspects of ethical issues with commendable care and pro-fessionalism. But not all governing bodies attract such commendation. For example, the proud but self-congratulatory boast of the Law Society of Scotland in the 1980s as to inculcating and maintaining the allegedly high ethical standards of its members that 'No one does it better' appears on the evidence of solicitor defalcation, of complaints statistics, of Lay Observers Annual Reports and particular Opinions, and of ethics scandals involving Scottish solicitors, the very opposite of the truth and is about as convincing as the recurrent fanatical but fanciful claim that Scotland is going to win the (soccer) World Cup. But even in the case of a model law society, the public perception, perhaps inevitably, is of lawyers protecting their own:

> Cattle duffers on a jury may be honest men enough
> But they're bound to visit lightly sins of those who cattle duff
> (*Melbourne Punch*, 15 July 1886).

Compromising fundamental principles of natural justice certainly calls for greater and more cogent justification than lawyers have ever offered in defence of self-regulation. The standard argument offered is that non-lawyers simply do not and cannot be expected to understand the complex nature of law and legal practice and to subject lawyers to assessment by

66

non-lawyers would be unfair. That is easily refuted by pointing to philosophers who write penetrating and scholarly works on and about law without the benefit either of a law degree or any direct experience of legal practice or to those who have acted as lay observers or legal services ombudsmen who by statute must not be lawyers yet who have included among their number individuals whose particular Opinions and Annual Reports exhibit the penetrating insight, fair-mindedness, cogent reasoning, and clarity of expression that one legitimately expects but does not always find in the correspondence and reports of lawyers and their lawyer-regulators. The mystification of their craft as something beyond the capacity of non-lawyers to understand is not merely arrogant; it is, ultimately, a refusal by lawyers to account for their conduct. And if it is unfair for non-lawyers to judge lawyers it must be unfair, too, for lawyers to judge non-lawyers.

Non-lawyer observers and ombudsmen

In Britain governments have recognised that self-regulation by lawyers may result in self-protection of lawyers and a compromise was reached whereby the handling by the (English) Law Society and by the Law Society of Scotland of complaints made by members of the public about solicitors would be open to review by a non-lawyer appointed by government, rather quaintly called 'the Lay Observer'. Anyone dissatisfied with the handling of a complaint about a solicitor was provided with a statutory right to refer the matter to the Lay Observer and the Lay Observer was granted statutory powers to facilitate review of the handling of complaints, including access to Law Society files.

Among these Lay Observers duties, the duty annually to report is significant in that for about fifteen years or so annual reports have been prepared and laid before Parliament. These give an insight into the handling of complaints by the law societies and contain statistical records invaluable to any assessment of the performance of the law societies that aspires to a degree of objectivity. Such reports contain detailed accounts of cases which have caused difficulty and provide for the applied ethicist a useful source of practical examples and ethical controversy. Because this institutional arrangement has been copied in some Commonwealth jurisdictions, comparative study, essential to any critical assessment of how any one law society is actually performing, is also facilitated by the existence of such reports. Since some American jurisdictions have a parallel officer, called the 'State Monitor', a wide range of materials and issues can be accessed.

Such reports also facilitate assessment of a law societys performance over time. Here the Scottish reports reveal some deep divisions between the views of the Lay Observer and the Law Society of Scotland and Lay Observer recommendations have been frequently rejected. Indeed, despite the heroic efforts of some individual Lay Observers, it is not easy to be at all confident that there has been any significant improvement in the handling of complaints or in the ethical quality of the conduct of solicitors in Scotland. Understandably there has been much criticism of these institutional arrangements and it has been seriously doubted whether self-regulation can be made to work, even with the involvement of a Lay Observer (New South Wales Law Reform Commission, 1992)

In Britain, criticism and dissatisfaction has led to a change not only of name but also in the powers and jurisdictions of the observers. The (English) Legal Services Ombudsman and the Scottish Legal Services Ombudsman now have power to review handling of complaints about a wider range of professional providers of legal services and advice, including barristers in England and advocates in Scotland, and powers to award compensation and to institute disciplinary proceedings where a law society has not done so. It is still rather early to assess the significance of these changes but early signs and transitional experience are not encouraging.

The statistics of complaints made to law societies continue to give cause for concern. So overwhelmed has the (English) Solicitors Complaints Bureau found itself that, in an effort to reduce the volume of complaints, the (English) Law Society imposed a duty on law firms to provide an in-house complaints procedure and commended conciliation as a means of dealing with client complaints. It is reported that many law firms have been slow to implement these innovations and that the Solicitors Complaints Bureau will have to 'get tough' (*The Times*, 27 March 1993).

In Scotland, the combined intellectual power and legal skills of the Law Society of Scotland (which very actively lobbied Parliament, and with considerable success in terms of the interests of Scottish solicitors), the Scottish Office, and the Parliamentary Draftsman could not prevent the amending legislation, despite the obvious intention to strengthen the position of those aggrieved with the conduct of solicitors, depriving about 130 individuals of their preexisting statutory right to refer the handling of their complaints by the Law Society of Scotland to an independent government appointee. This is a spectacular failure of legislative intent and, given (at the time of writing) that the Scottish Office apparently intends to do nothing to rectify the defect, it also indicates a lack of moral purpose. Those 130 individuals who, on their own view of the matter have each been ill served, first, by a Scottish solicitor and, secondly, by the Law Society of Scotland have, on any view of the matter, thirdly, been ill served and, apparently, abandoned by government.

Even dismissing transitional difficulties and the large backlog of cases that had a team of auxiliary temporary Lay Observers beavering away in England to reduce the business to manageable proportions for the incoming Legal Services Ombudsman, the current institutional arrangements fail to satisfy even such minimalist criteria for accountability as accessibility, openness and speed. Anyone aggrieved with the conduct of a lawyer should have early access to an intelligible and user-friendly process. As it is, even after the recent round of reforms in Britain, those aggrieved with the conduct of a lawyer have to cope with the sometimes glacial pace of response exhibited by the Solicitors Complaints Bureau and the Complaints Office of the Law Society of Scotland, with cumbersome administrative and committee procedures and, not infrequently, adversarialism and wholly inappropriate levels of hostility. It may take many months, sometimes over a year, before a person aggrieved receives a final answer from the regulators.

In such circumstances, tinkering with the office of Lay Observer or Legal Services Ombudsman, however admirable individual incumbents may be, holds out only limited prospects of significant amelioration, especially given the wholly inadequate resources provided by governments and the part-time nature of the office in several jurisdictions. What is urgently required, and what successive governments in Britain have failed to address, is the creation of a permanent Legal Services Commission, adequately staffed and properly funded, by a levy on lawyers if necessary.

Lawyers' ethics and codes of conduct

Turning back from the problem of natural justice inherent in self-regulation to the problem of definition, it is no easy matter to state the nature and content of lawyers' ethics. To some experienced lawyers even the attempt is misconceived (Phillips, 1990, p. 65). Lawyers' ethics in their view cannot be embodied in a code of duties but are exhibited in the virtues of the good lawyer and communicated from the experienced to the inexperienced not by precept but by example. Although lawyers' ethics, like Platonic justice, cannot be captured in words or rules, just like the philosopher encountering justice, the experienced lawyer can instantly and intuitively recognize ethically right and ethically wrong conduct. Such experienced lawyers apply and advocate the 'blush test' as moral litmus — only if it makes an experienced practitioner blush is the conduct in question morally beyond the pale.[8]

Notwithstanding the attractions of this view of the lawyer as an experienced practitioner of refined and well developed moral sensitivity, recent practice in most common law jurisdictions has been to promulgate codes of ethics. It is early days to assess the impact of these infant codes as effective guides for professional conduct and as common and accessible standards for critical or disciplinary reaction when breached but it is already plain that they vary greatly in length, detail, precision, analytical rigour, internal coherence, and seriousness of purpose.

For example, the Scottish code for solicitors, promulgated in 1989, is decidedly minimalist and runs to only two pages, stating ten principles, often in broad aspirational language, with little or nothing by way of supportive commentary. It contrasts markedly with the English Guide to Professional Conduct with is very extensive, rich in detail, commentary, example, and special — morally perplexing — cases, e.g. child abuse. Some may see in the Scottish code an instance of the Scottish genius for broadly worded general principles such as characterized Acts of the Scottish Parliament prior to 1707 in direct contradistinction to the wordy, detailed English approach to legislation, but judged solely in terms of assisting non-lawyers assess the conformity of lawyers conduct to the current ethics of their chosen profession, the English code and commentaries are streets ahead. In the light of the historical reluctance exhibited by the Law Society of Scotland to promulgate any code at all, it is difficult successfully to extirpate the suspicion that the 1989 code was more a cosmetic exercise in public relations than any serious attempt to provide publicly accessible and binding standards of lawyer conduct and accountability.

Even where a code is a good faith effort conscientiously to address the wide range of moral perplexity that assails lawyers in current society in accessible language, the voluntary 'in-house' nature of code generation, interpretation and implementation calls for review. It should not be possible, as it is at present, for a law society to apply its code differently to members according as they are sole practitioners or partners in large firms or worse, as has been alleged in Scotland, to discriminate against some lawyers on religious grounds. Nor should it be possible for a law society to choose not to apply its code at all in a particular case where a well founded complaint has been made.

The conduct of a law society is, of course, open to challenge in the courts and individuals dissatisfied with a law societys handling of a complaint may attempt to bring the matter before a statutory disciplinary tribunal. Both these options, however, involve complex and potentially expensive legal procedures which intimidate and which are operated by lawyers. It is difficult, therefore, for an aggrieved member of the public, dissatisfied with a law society's handling of a complaint, to have confidence in or be comfortable with the existing institutions and procedures and easy to understand why so many who have complained to a law society about a lawyers conduct are left only with feelings of frustration and alienation. It is easy, too, to understand the public's perception that lawyers simply are not accountable in any meaningful sense.

The problems of definition, of natural justice, and of alienation may be eased by codification and publication of professional standards and duties within a statutory framework and by substantially increased non-lawyer participation in sustaining and developing acceptable ethical standards and conduct through the establishment of an adequately funded and staffed Legal Services Commission. As a first step, the British government should set up an inquiry into the ethics and accountability of the legal professions.

The current thinking underlying accountability regimes for lawyers is still that self-regulation can be made to work. Accordingly, in response to public dissatisfaction, governments have granted law societies more statutory powers but a grant of such powers carries no guarantee that they will be used for the purposes or in the manner that the government contemplated and intended. Law societies are in a difficult position in that they have professional association duties to their membership and duties to the public at large. Whilst it may be possible to reconcile these duties there is a standing risk that a law society, given its membership and structure, will give more weight to the interests of its members than to the interests of the public. A society not fully committed to its duties to the public and zealously committed to its duties to its members may develop stratagems for blunting and diverting criticisms and for disposing of complaints. In such circumstances the accountability of lawyers is eroded and complaints procedures merely a sorry sham.

It is a commonplace in legal studies that in disputes experience impacts on outcomes. A repeat-player will usually outperform a one-off participant (Galanter, 1974, p. 9). Plainly institutional litigants have advantages in disputes with citizens and corporations have advantages over consumers. In like manner lawyers have such advantages over clients that the playing field requires some levelling. Law societies are not, and given their necessary commitment to their members cannot ever be, neutral adjudicators of lawyer-client disputes.

The office of lay observer/legal services ombudsman is one institutional attempt to neutralize inequalities. The history and development of that office, particularly in recent years in Britain, reveals a transformation from its origins as a toothless observer reporting to government to its present condition as an altogether more interventionist and active participant in the resolution of disputes arising out of complaints from clients and non-clients about the conduct of lawyers and lawyer-regulators. The recent renaming and the empowering of the office does not, in my submission, complete the transformative process.

One would expect a progressive transference of complaints handling from law societies to ombudsmen, an increased attention by ombudsmen

71

to questions of substance rather than of procedure, and to securing an outcome acceptable to the person aggrieved by the conduct of the lawyer. At the same time one would expect law societies to devote increasing effort to the dissemination and inculcation of ethical standards, through promulgation of codes and compulsory continuing legal education programmes. In short, one would expect the ombudsmen to be concerned primarily with compensatory justice for individuals aggrieved and the governing bodies of the legal professions to be concerned primarily with the standing of the professions and corrective justice for professional miscreants.

Immanent in that transformation is a rapidly escalating workload for legal services ombudsmen and an emerging need greatly to expand the institution from a small scale, possibly part-time, activity to a permanent standing commission, fully equipped with the powers necessary to its function, adequately staffed and properly funded. In Queensland, the Criminal Justice Commission was conceived as an independent means of sustaining ethical standards in police work and public life and investigating all manner of complaints of misconduct and corruption. The Legal Services Commission is here conceived as a parallel institution providing independent review of the conduct of lawyers and lawyer-regulators, investigating complaints and reconciling the internal ethics of the legal professions with the needs, expectations and values of the public. Above all, such a Commission would call lawyers, individually and collectively, to account.

Openness and confidentiality

Even if these proposals found favour and were implemented serious problems about lawyer accountability remain. It is sometimes argued that there is a moral or political duty to open oneself up to scrutiny and to account for ones conduct and position at least where one enjoys differential status or privilege as compared with other members of society. Bruce Ackerman (1980, 1983), for example, offers an intriguing defence of liberalism as (constrained) dialogue where power-holders are obliged to offer a justification when challenged. Certain justificatory moves are ruled out: the power-holder cannot appeal to privileged access to moral truth nor to any innate moral superiority, nor can the challenge simply be suppressed, and if the conversation ends in silence the power-holder loses the argument. Such liberalism entails or requires substantial freedom of information.

Lawyers enjoy privileged status in the law-making enterprise. They are members of the interpretative community that determines the meaning and scope of the rules and principles that apply to all and they are the gatekeepers of the institutions that formally determine such meanings. However, the conduct of lawyers is actually shrouded in secrecy. Professionally lawyers are ethically and legally bound by stringent requirements of confidentiality (Tur, 1992). There are several standard examples in the international literature of lawyers ethics (Kaplan, 1988; Chamberlain, 1976). The following are the words of a Scottish solicitor:

> During the year of 1973, and frequently in the next two years, a murderer would appear in my office, always unannounced, never by appointment, and he would see only me. He would sit across the desk from me, tormenting me — although, in fairness, this was not his purpose — with more and more of his dark and dramatic secret.
>
> He and another man had been responsible for the murder of an elderly Jewish woman during a robbery at her bungalow home some four years earlier. Neither of them had been caught, although the man in front of me had escaped capture by the proverbial whisker. Now here he was, sitting in my office as a client, slowly dripping more and more information that an innocent man, Patrick Meehan, had been jailed for that murder.
>
> Indeed he was saying more than that ... he was virtually telling me that he was the murderer.
>
> And I was helpless! Because of a strict rule of confidentiality between solicitor and client, I could do nothing about it — while Meehan, also a client of mine, languished in jail.
>
> Call it, if you will a golden rule that cannot be broken, rather like that of a confessor in the Roman Catholic Church. He, too, can never divulge anything told to him within the walls of the confessional. For three years I was well and truly saddled with the crushing burden of knowing that such confidences between solicitor and client are inviolable for the lifetime of the client (Beltrami, 1989, p. 19).

Confidentiality itself raises no novel problems for the moral philosopher. If information is received or imparted in circumstances of confidentiality then there is a moral obligation not to divulge that information to others. Whether that obligation is absolute or defeasible varies according to competing theories of the nature of moral obligation and what circumstances actually will defeat the moral obligation of confidentiality also varies according to competing theories. All that is plain sailing but when professional ethics intrude, serious complications arise.

Journalists frequently complain that theirs is the only profession whose members may be imprisoned for adhering to the requirement of their professional ethics. A journalist who will not reveal the identity of a source when required to do so by a court faces a very real risk of imprisonment (*The Courier-Mail*, [Brisbane] May 1 1993; *The Weekend Australian*, May 8-9 1993). The law has adopted a defeasible conception of confidentiality in respect of journalists and courts will require journalists to breach confidentiality where (in the courts opinion) the public interest so requires.

In contrast, however, lawyers cannot be compelled by a court to disclose confidential information. Lord Denning put it thus:

> The only profession I know which is given a privilege from disclosing information to a court of law is the legal profession, and then it is not the privilege of the lawyer but of his client. Take the clergyman, the banker or the medical man. None of these is entitled to refuse to answer when directed to by a judge (*Attorney-General v Mulholland and Foster*, [1963], 2 QBD 477, 491).

This seriously limits the extent to which lawyers can open themselves up to external scrutiny. The generally recognised professional duty of confidentiality and legal professional privilege impact on the accountability of lawyers. If, putting the matter at its very strongest, the professional duty of confidentiality applies to any and all information acquired by lawyers in the course of their practice then some information relevant to judgements about lawyer conduct will be subject to that professional duty, hidden from view on ethical grounds, and unlikely to be readily available either to official or unofficial scrutineers. More generally, confidentiality and privilege are obviously open to abuse and exploitation by unscrupulous clients and unethical lawyers alike secure in the knowledge that they are unlikely to be called to account for activities which by their very nature must and will be kept secret.

Where clients complain about the conduct of their own lawyers, confidentiality and privilege are clearly waived by implication if not expressly, but where clients are content with the conduct of their lawyers, even though that conduct may be professionally unethical, crucial information is protected by the ethical duty of confidentiality and the legal doctrine of privilege and investigation of third party complaints may be hampered by the lawyers invocation of confidentiality and privilege. Only one law society that I have researched has accepted this argument.[9] Other societies have resolutely litigated the point against their own recalcitrant members and won, the courts holding that the public interest in the investigation of lawyer misconduct overrides the public interest arguments in favour of legal professional privilege.[10] However the outcome of such cases is that whereas client confidentiality and legal privilege may be trumped by virtue of powers conferred on governing bodies by relevant

74

legal practitioner legislation, and for the related purpose of disciplinary proceedings, the information retains its confidential and privileged status for all other purposes. Accordingly, information crucial to an informed assessment of the ethical quality of lawyering remains hidden from public view and one is left only with lawyers accountability to lawyers.

Confidentiality and privilege are obviously controversial because it seems that lawyers can hide behind them to avoid scrutiny and to render immoral assistance to 'obviously' wicked and guilty clients. But one cannot simply abolish privilege even though it does provide cover for rogue solicitors: ' ... if communications between legal advisers and their clients were subject to compulsory disclosure in litigation, civil or criminal, there would be a restriction, serious in many cases, upon the freedom with which advice or representations could be given or sought' (*Baker v Campbell* (1983), 57 ALJR 749, 49 ALR 385 (HC) per Dawson J). In such circumstances one cannot seek advice from a legal adviser confident that this will not turn out to ones disadvantage.

Clearly communications between client and lawyer require protection from compulsory disclosure if legal advice is to be available at all. No rational person would consult a lawyer if consultation rendered conviction or liability more rather than less likely. It follows that calls for greater openness to facilitate greater accountability, however justified these may be from an external ethical perspective, generate very real difficulties for the legal profession, both individually and collectively, because it challenges central features of the lawyer-client relationship such as mutual trust and confidence. The difficulty, then, with external ethical criticism of the conduct of lawyers is that it entails that they should not be lawyers. From such external ethical perspectives, 'lawyers' ethics' would appear to be a contradiction in terms.

Costs and the personal liability of lawyers

Concern with lawyers ethics is driven in part by perceptions of unconscionable delays and disproportionate costs. As to costs, in England, some individual solicitors may find themselves personally liable under Order 62, rule 11 of the Rules of the Supreme Court where costs have been incurred improperly or unreasonably or have been wasted by the solicitors failure to conduct the proceedings with reasonable competence and expedition (*Orchard v S.E. Electricity Board*, [1987] 1 All E R 95; *Sinclair-Jones v Kay* [1988] 1 All E R 611; *Gupta v Comer* [1991] 1 All E R 289). Individual lawyers (in Britain, only solicitors) may find themselves financially accountable to the court if costs have been generated improperly by their conduct of the case and if the other side makes the appropriate application at the appropriate time. Clearly Order 62 rule 11 has considerable potential to discourage lawyers from running up costs improperly or unreasonably. However its impact depends crucially upon opposing lawyers making the necessary applications and for a cluster of fairly obvious reasons that is unlikely to happen except in fairly exceptional circumstances. For that reason Order 62 rule 11 is apt to curtail only the grosser forms of cost padding and creative billing.

Collective accountability of the legal professions?

Among the difficulties generated by external ethical criticism is whether such criticism, if warranted at all, is more appropriately directed towards individual lawyers or to lawyers collectively. Individual lawyers are accountable, be it ever so weakly, for their conduct to their professional bodies and to the courts. But it may be that lawyers acting impeccably judged by the current ethics of their profession nonetheless generate alarming costs. Indeed, it is clear that if two lawyers zealously bend their skill and energy to the realization of the conflicting objectives of their two clients the costs may be out of all proportion to the subject matter, as for example where the legal costs entirely consume the property in dispute between divorcing parties. 'The situation occurs again and again when the court finds itself unable to make appropriate provision for the parties and their children because of their liability for legal costs and it is a matter of the gravest concern to all judges' (*Evans v Evans*, [1990], 1 FLR 319, 321, per Booth J). Grave though their concern may be, the judges have not been able to do very much about it except in a few cases where there has been a serious dereliction of duty and if the lawyers conduct has been so inexcusable as to merit reproof. In the ordinary run of cases, where lawyers zealously pursue the conflicting interests of their clients, very considerable costs may be run up without either lawyer deserving reproof. Indeed, each lawyer could point to a professional ethical duty zealously to pursue the interests of each client.

The structure of the adversarial system and the nature of lawyers duties to clients can lead to unnecessarily long and complex trials and great delay, and some powerful voices have recently expressed criticism of excessive zeal. In *Ashmore v Corporation of Lloyds* (1992), Lord Roskill observes that 'the writ in this case was issued nearly five years ago in the Commercial Court' and observes the irony that when the 'Commercial List was introduced into the Queens Bench Division of the High Court its purpose was to facilitate speedy trial of commercial disputes in the simplest manner'. Notwithstanding that tradition,

[t]he Court of Appeal appear to have taken the view that the plaintiffs were entitled of right to have their case tried to conclusion in such manner as they thought fit and if necessary after all the evidence on both sides has been adduced. With great respect, I emphatically disagree. In the Commercial Court and indeed in any trial court it is the trial judge who has control of the proceedings. It is part of his duty to identify the crucial issues and to see they are tried as expeditiously as possible. It is the duty of the advisers of the parties to assist the trial judge in carrying out his duty. Litigants are not entitled to the uncontrolled use of a trial judge's time. Other litigants await their turn. Litigants are only entitled to so much of the trial judges time as is necessary for the proper determination of the relevant issues (WLR 446, 448)

Lord Templeman had already commented in an earlier case (*Banque Keyser Ullmann SA v Skandia (UK) Insurance Co. Ltd*, [1991] 2 A C 249, 280) on proceedings in which some or all of the litigants indulge in over-elaboration and the resultant difficulties for judges at all levels. In *Ashmore v Corporation of Lloyds* (1992) he returned to that theme:

The parties and particularly their legal advisers in any litigation are under a duty to co-operate with the court by chronological, brief and consistent pleadings which define the issues and leave the judge to draw his own conclusions about the merits when he hears the case. It is the duty of counsel to assist the judge by simplification and concentration and not to advance a multitude of ingenious arguments in the hope that out of ten bad points the judge will be capable of fashioning a winner. In nearly all cases the correct procedure works perfectly well. But there has been a tendency in some cases for legal advisers, pressed by their clients, to make every point conceivable and inconceivable without judgement or discrimination.

These are strong words, very highly critical of some practitioners. Lawyers, as officers of the court and of justice, have a duty to reject instructions from clients calculated to exploit, prejudice, or thwart the orderly and proper processes of litigation (*Grosvenor (Mayfair) Estates Ltd v Raja, The Times*, November 2 1990).

The structure of the adversarial system and the nature of lawyers duties to clients also leads to economic madness. *In re W (a Minor)* (1993)

the costs, in accordance with figures furnished by counsel in court or supplied by the local authority at the hearing were: (i) legal costs, borne in part by the Legal Aid Fund and in part by the local authority, £1 million approximately; (ii) in-house costs of the local authority's social service and legal departments, £1 million approximately. On top of those, there were the additional unquantified but no doubt very substantial costs of abortive criminal proceedings involving the father and borne in part on criminal legal aid and in part by the prosecuting authorities (*The Times*, March 23, 1993)

Lord Justice Hirst commented that 'it was right that these figures should be known to the public' and stated that 'it would not necessarily be right to conclude that money had been culpably wasted ... But it had manifestly to be a matter of acute public concern that the present system of conducting such cases could result in such apparently profligate expenditure of public funds'. It would be comforting to be able to explain these extraordinary costs as due to some wrongdoing by those conducting the case but just suppose that the lawyers involved did nothing particularly out of the ordinary and that there was no serious dereliction of duty deserving reproof. On these suppositions criticism for the apparently profligate expenditure cannot be directed at the individual lawyers but must be diverted towards 'the system'.

Whereas individual lawyers cannot reasonably be blamed for the failings of the system, lawyers collectively have an obvious responsibility yet, despite widespread recognition of duties of 'civic professionalism' such as are included in the Scottish code, and a rather ill defined expectation of pro bono work in many jurisdictions, lawyers collectively appear to be doing nothing or little about the costs explosion as illustrated by *In re W (a Minor)* — and examples can be multiplied — nor is it clear that it is in the collective interests of lawyers that much be done. Of course government interest is excited where public funds are involved but the problem is much wider in that a significant portion of public and private resources are consumed in fruitless litigation and lawyering.

Two-point-something million pounds sterling is a shocking sum, whatever the complexities of the case and the merits of the opposing arguments. It is certainly 'right that these figures should be known to the public', but such knowledge of itself moves nothing. One also needs to know how such costs accumulated and that requires access to information not available in the law reports and, perhaps, not available at all because of confidentiality and privilege. A thorough, detailed case study is required before one can attribute responsibility and propose reform. Ideally, one would wish to interview some of the participants. *In re W (a Minor)* is only one case. To generate practicable reform proposals one would need to access a critical mass of materials rather than one isolated case, however spectacular. It also has to be decided who is to conduct such research, report, and monitor progress and whether extraordinary statutory powers are necessary in order to facilitate thorough investigation.

Such conspicuous consumption of resources seems properly a matter of collective responsibility for which the legal profession as a whole must answer. However, unless professional misconduct is alleged such cases would not in the normal course of business come before the governing bodies of the legal profession for investigation. Even if professional misconduct was alleged, any investigation conducted by or for a legal profession governing body would be limited to determining whether there was a breach of professional ethics, not whether costs blow-outs were a probable or certain result of lawyers zealously pursuing clients interests, nor whether current ethical imperatives should be revised. Accordingly such cases occur without any proper scrutiny or review by the legal professions collectively nor are the governing bodies of these professions called on to explain and justify the excessive consumption of public and private resources. From time to time judges express grave concern and periodically the media indignantly highlight particularly extreme instances of costs madness but the fundamental issues simply are not addressed.

At present, indeed, there is no institutional mechanism to structure the dialogue and to mediate between lawyers collectively and society as a whole. Hence the plea in this paper for a Legal Services Commission to which the governing bodies of the legal professions must account for the social and economic impact of their enterprises. The deep crisis in legal services calls for immediate government action. Together with a Legal Services Commission, I advocate statutorily backed codes of conduct, greatly increased non-lawyer participation, and compulsory continuing legal education for practitioners, including a compulsory ethics component and mandatory ethics teaching in law degree courses.

Virtuous lawyers

The prevailing conception of the 'good lawyer' is instrumentalist. An alternative conception might be developed in terms of virtue. Given some basic assumptions about the necessary indeterminacy of and conflicts among legal rules and principles there is more or less room, depending on circumstances, at the point of application for choice. Since the legal system makes contact with peoples lives at least sometimes, perhaps often, through the mediation of lawyers, how these lawyers understand, interpret and apply the law becomes very important and their choices at the point of law application have privileged status. If lawyers approach their tasks critically, sensitively and imaginatively, theirs is a creative, developmental role. Of course, there are no guarantees that these lawyers will apply their ingenuity to the production of 'good' outcomes. Given the contested and polar context of law application at least some lawyers, some of the time, will be seeking to produce outcomes that some members of society, perhaps a minority, would regard as morally problematic. In this, the lawyer is no different from the non-lawyer. Some non-lawyers, too, seek outcomes that some members of society, perhaps a minority, would regard as morally problematic.

The lawyers representative role is to present the clients case in the best possible light, uninfluenced by any personal view of the clients objectives, and to mediate apparent conflict between the clients objectives and the law by seeking an arguable reading of the law which accommodates the client's objectives or an approximation thereto. In this way, the law is exposed to constant critical review at the edges and tends to accommodate the widest possible range of diverse objectives. The lawyer here acts as a liberator and as a powerful friend of moral autonomy (Fried, 1986, p. 132). Of course the objectives of some clients may be so at odds with the moral content of the law as to be beyond the ability even of the most ingenious lawyer to accommodate and it is the lawyers ethical duty in such circumstances so to advise the client. Ethically, the lawyer may not advise clients as to ways in which unlawful purposes may be achieved but the lawyer can seek to reconcile the clients objectives and the moral content of the law and advise clients as to ways in which they could pursue their objectives consistently with the law.

I submit that wide latitude has to be given to the prohibition on advice as to ways in which unlawful purposes may be achieved. Sometimes a lawyer may properly have to advise that existing law is open to challenge, either as formally defective, having been improperly made[11] or as substantively defective, being contrary to some relevant 'higher law' such as a bill of rights.

Consider the following newspaper item (*The Guardian*, 6 April 1993):

> Three gay men are to challenge Britains laws on the age of consent at the European Court of Human Rights in Strasbourg.
> ... [they] claim English and Scottish laws which criminalise sex between men where one is under 21, violate the European Convention on Human Rights.
> The age of 21, the highest in Europe, was fixed in 1967 when gay male sex was decriminalised. Heterosexual sex and sex between lesbians is lawful over the age of 16. Hundreds of men are prosecuted each year for under age gay sex ...

One of the men, a nineteen year old, is quoted as saying, 'We are not prepared to be treated as criminals any longer' and a Member of

Parliament is reported as having said, 'The existing law is unfair and has no moral or medical basis'. But at the time of writing consensual homosexual activities involving a man under 21 are contrary to the criminal law of England. A pending challenge in the European Court of Human Rights probably makes prosecution less likely in the meantime and to that extent legal advice, if any, received by the three men would have been perilously close to a suggestion as to how unlawful purposes might be achieved. Yet assisting clients such as these three men achieve their objectives despite the unsympathetic state of current law is exactly what is expected of the critical, sensitive and imaginative lawyer, with a creative approach to clients problems.

Lawyering is about sensitive judgement and contested claims. It is about individual freedom and social constraint, and it involves striking a balance between the demands made upon the citizen to conform as a team player and the individuals need for personal space — freedom under the law: 'Leave to live by no mans leave, underneath the Law' (Kipling, 1940, p. 297). Those who seek an education for life or who seek the educated life would do well, on this view of the subject, to study and even practise law. James Boyd White and Anthony Kronman have developed independent arguments that lead to a similar conclusion. The former plausibly suggests that the study of law is particularly apt to teach how to function as a member of an inherited culture whilst retaining individuality (White, 1985, pp. 49-59).

Kronman brilliantly develops the idea that any instrumental justification for the life of a lawyer whether couched in terms of income to be earned or in terms of social good to be done misses the point and presses on to offer an intrinsic justification (Kronman, 1987). The life of the lawyer, he suggests, is to be justified not by what it brings but by what it is. It is the life of the good judge. Judgement, for Kronman, is 'non-deductive' and 'non-intuitive' in that it has an argumentative dimension. Furthermore, judgement is constitutive in that the important life decisions one makes constitute, at least in part, the self that one becomes. Good judgement is concomitant with good character. The better ones judgement the greater the chances that one can live amicably with oneself and with others. One develops self-knowledge and character through the exercise of judgement.

Kronman clinches this argument with an account of the good lawyer whose work is marked by subtlety and imagination and, above all, wisdom. The characteristic virtue of the lawyer is, indeed, judgement. There is intrinsic worth in the life of the lawyer who lives up to the high ideals of the profession. The intrinsically good person is the person of developed and sound practical wisdom and a life in the law is conducive to such character. In short, to be a lawyer is a better way to be. Kronman is well aware of the modern tendencies, economic and education, that threaten the realization of the ideal. Indeed, much depends upon the economic, educational and professional culture surrounding the individual lawyer. That may be as destructive of the virtue that Kronman extols as supportive of it (Plato, [1973]; Tur, 1993).

'Virtuous lawyers' then, are to be valued not for the results that they can achieve but because of their intrinsic characteristic virtues; discriminating judgement, ethical sensitivity, creative imagination, and fidelity to a cluster of core values internal to law and lawyering. Virtuous lawyers may well be critical of clients objectives and may as readily seek to accommodate these to the law as vice versa by guiding and prompting clients but respect for and empowerment of the moral autonomy of clients limits the extent to which lawyers may substitute their own vision of the good for that of their clients either by stealth or pressure. Certainly virtuous lawyers may debate clients ends with clients just as a good and thoughtful friend may criticize and seek to persuade (Postema, 1986, p. 158). However, just as the advice and moral promptings of a best friend may be rejected, so a client may prove resistant to a lawyers moral discourse. At that stage, what the client wants is a given and the lawyers task is to find some way, if at all possible, of delivering, subject to the constraints imposed by and contained in the law.

Accordingly, the virtuous lawyer is in the balancing business, answering judgement calls about synthesizing conflicting objectives and values, such as justice and certainty, freedom and security, individualism and communitarianism, private objectives and public interest. This brings us to applied ethics and the interface between general moral principles and individual discretion. Reasonable individuals may reasonably differ, not only at the margins but also as to the basic commitments that constitute character, lifestyle, and objectives. Ethics is not about arriving at the one right answer. Nor can ethical problems be solved once and for all by legislative fiat. Judgement calls will always be made and there will always be a margin of individual appreciation in the application of rules and principles of law, procedure and ethics to the concrete and particular facts of real-life circumstances.

From the perspective of the virtuous lawyer, one can only have limited enthusiasm for codes of ethics for lawyers unless such a code is conceived of as a body of general principles and standards which function as guidelines rather than as all-or-nothing rules purporting exhaustively to predetermine outcomes and eliminate the need for engaged reflection and conscientious decision making at the point of application. Codification of lawyers ethics, much as it is to be applauded as an exercise in communication and accountability, carries with it a risk that the black letter of the codes will substitute for the critical reflection of the engaged practitioner. I believe that lawyering in all its forms makes judgement calls and I further believe that these calls are necessarily ethical, calling upon the lawyer conscientiously to address questions of right and wrong in a bewildering range of particular circumstances. No code can predetermine such questions though codes can, and do, articulate (some of) the principles and values that are relevant in the deliberations of the virtuous lawyer. A life in the law is, necessarily, an adventure in applied ethics.

Lawyers ethics matter; not simply to lawyers, but to everyone because erosion of lawyers ethical standards rebounds upon the quality of the criminal and civil justice systems and ultimately upon the quality of life. Lawyers ethics matter too, not only to practising lawyers but also, and importantly, to law teachers who not only must convey some sense of the process values of the law and of the ethical standards essential to good lawyering, but also something of the disciplined creativity and moral imagination of virtuous lawyering despite the deadening, depersonalising fixity of black letter legalism.

Anglo-American legal systems face a crisis in legal services. For most citizens, the law is beyond reach. Those who believe that they can afford legal services are frequently shocked to discover the real cost. Legal aid budgets are in disarray and provide support only for limited numbers. Corporate lawyering consumes millions annually. Beyond cost, there are the laws delays. Beyond cost and delay there is a concern that despite the investment of all that time and money the results achieved are unsatisfactory. In such circumstances it is easy to condemn individual lawyers for their contribution to the crisis, and some individual lawyers richly deserve blame, but in principle such condemnation is unfair in that the difficulties are generated at a different level.

The seeds of economic blow-out are contained within the standard conception of the lawyers role in an adversarial system and reinforced by professional ethics. Paradoxically, zealous adherence to professional ethics can sometimes rebound adversely on the public interest. It is not enough, important as it is, to consider whether lawyers are acting in accordance with the standards and values of their profession; one must also ask whether compliance with professional ethics fosters or frustrates the common good. In general, lawyers have a duty to explore every issue, put every argument, raise every question, and employ every legal resource that will assist their clients. Two opposing lawyers, acting conscientiously in accordance with these requirements even in a relatively simple matter will necessarily generate substantial costs for their clients, without any cost-padding or overcharging. Cost-padding and overcharging are problems *within* lawyers ethics (and as such are dealt with, more or less adequately, by governing bodies according to established practices and procedures[12] Economic blow-out is a problem *with* lawyers ethics (and appears not to be dealt with by any institution).

I have suggested that virtuous lawyers are in the balancing business, answering judgement calls about synthesizing conflicting objectives and values. There is an obvious social need to reconcile the conflicting tendencies of openness and confidentiality, of service and cost, and of accountability and independence, and virtuous lawyers should play their part in that endeavour, both individually and collectively through their societies and governing bodies. But there is also an obvious need for government to set in place appropriate institutional arrangements, and for law teachers and continuing legal education directors creatively to devise effective programmes suited to these tasks.

Notes

1. *Spaulding v Zimmerman* 116 NW 2d 704 (1962) Supreme Court of Minnesota; withholding a medical report also features in *W v Egdell* [1989] 1 All E R 1089. In some cases, however, preexisting medical reports will be available to the courts; see *Dunn v British Coal Corporation, The Times*, 5 March 1993 and *O'Sullivans v Herdmans Ltd* (1987) 1 WLR 1047.

2. See Wasserstrom, Richard (1986), 'Lawyers as Professionals: Some Moral Issues' in Davis, Michael and Elliston, Frederick A. (eds), *Ethics and the Legal Profession*, Prometheus Books, New York, p.114 and the editors comments at p.110.

3. Rutherford, Andrew (1993), *Criminal Justice and the Pursuit of Decency* OUP, Oxford, pp. 87-88: 'You can become very isolated if you take on a cause of this nature. My professional brethren were never overtly hostile to me, but there came a point where they felt that I had done enough and that I was being fanatical to continue. That was where we started to part company on what was important so far as principles were concerned. I learnt paranoia and what it is like to be followed, to have my office burgled, and to be under surveillance. I have an MI5 bug file and a profile on the Lisburn computer. I have been branded as having espoused the Republican cause simply because I was prepared to do what I was professionally obliged to do, which was to offer legal services to individuals who stood charged with an offence'. The same solicitor is reported, at p. 47, as saying, 'I had a telephone call from the magistrates' court asking if I wanted a legal aid certificate for one of the 'Guildford bombers' and I said that it should go to one of the bigger people because a case of that magnitude would monopolise me. They rang back a couple of hours later saying nobody else would take the legal aid certificate. I said that was ridiculous and we have got to do it if

the legal aid certificate is on offer. I rang the police station and said that I had been offered the legal aid certificate and wanted to see my client. There was a hostile atmosphere on the telephone and they said that they would ring back'.

4. See, for example, *Re Milte* (1992) A C L Rep 250 SA 1, where eight partners in a firm of solicitors induced clients to pay in cash so as to avoid declaring taxable income. The scheme had run for three years and was discovered by chance. Each had been convicted of defrauding the Commonwealth and all were struck off.

5. See, for example, *Griffiths v Dawson & Co* (5 April 1993), 'A solicitor, acting for a wife who was being divorced on the ground of separation after a long marriage to a man in pensionable employment, was negligent if he failed to make an application under section 10 of the Matrimonial Causes Act, 1973 to protect the wife's financial position', *The Times*.

6. *R v Brown & Others* (1993) 2 All E R 75 and see *Prothonotary of the Supreme Court NSW v Chapman* [1993] A C L rep 250 NSW 2 where, a solicitor who had been convicted for keeping a brothel was reprimanded by the court.

7. See, for example, *Report of a Commission of Inquiry into Possible Illegal Activities and Associated Police Misconduct*, (G.E. Fitzgerald QC, Chairman), 3 July 1989, leading to the establishment of the Criminal Justice Commission in Queensland. Section 9.2.3. deals with 'The Failure of the Police Complaints Tribunal'. Among the comments made, the Commission observed: 'Despite its title, the Tribunals role is wholly dependent on the very institution into which it is meant to be inquiring... In practical terms, the investigation of police is still in the hands of police officers'. Recommendation C II 2 is that 'the Police Complaints Tribunal be abolished'.

8. Freedman, Monroe H. (1975), *Lawyers' Ethics in an Adversary System*, New York, vii, remarks that he 'learned virtually nothing about legal ethics while in law school' and that the ethical difficulties of legal practice were avoided either by comments such as, 'A lawyer should never do anything that a gentleman would not do' — the blush test — or by '... issuing statements or codifications of rules of conduct in such a way as to give lip-service to basic systemic values, while ignoring the fact that some of these values are fundamentally at odds with each other'.

9. Solicitor's letter dated May 31, 1991 to the Law Society of Scotland, 'We consider ... that the powers conferred on the Law Society [of Scotland] under Section 42C [of the Solicitors (Scotland) Act, 1980, as amended] do not innovate on the general law ... of ... solicitor-client confidentiality ... If it is the Law Society [of Scotland]s intention

to pursue the matter to the Court please note that ... it will be our intention to instruct Counsel ... with a view to the Courts determining whether Section 42C entitles the Law Society [of Scotland] to recover the documents specified in the notice'.

10. For example, in England, *Parry-Jones v The Law Society* [1968] 1 All E R 179; in New South Wales, *A Solicitor v The Law Society of New South Wales & Anor* (in the Supreme Court of New South Wales, No 18475 of 1987, unreported, 24 page transcript of judgement supplied to author by the Law Society of New South Wales); and in the Northern Territory of Australia, *Rogerson v Law Society of the Northern Territory* (1991) 1 NTLR 100

11. (6 May 1993), *Courier-Mail*, 'Every by-law passed by the Brisbane City Council in the past 15 years has been thrown into legal doubt because of an embarrassing bureaucratic error'. The Local Government Minister is reported as saying that no one should try a court challenge to the by-laws because (retrospective) legislation would be introduced into Parliament to rectify the error. Such circumstances are fraught with legal and ethical difficulties.

12. As illustrative see Solicitors Disciplinary Tribunal Case No. 39 of February 2, 1993 (April 1993), Solicitor 'X' admitted several instances of overcharging, e.g. $2,050 instead of $609, $2,943 instead of $659, and $1,328.25 instead of $506.25., reported in the Queensland Law Society Journal, pp. 192-193.

References

Ackerman, Bruce (1980), *Social Justice in the Liberal State*, UP, Yale and (1983), *Reconstructing American Law* UP, Harvard.

Beltrami, Joe (1989), *A Deadly Innocence*, Mainstream Publishing.

Council of the Law Society of Scotland v J, (1991), S L T 662

Chamberlain, J.F. (1976) 'Confidentiality and the Case of Robert Garrow's Lawyers', 25 *Buff L Rev* 221.

Fried, Charles (1986), 'The Lawyer as Friend' in Davis and Elliston, (eds), *Ethics and the Legal Profession*, Prometheus Books, New York, p.132

Galanter, Marc (1974), 'Why the 'Haves' Come Out Ahead: Speculations on the Limits of Legal Change', *Law and Society Review*, No 1, 95.

Kaplan, David (25 January 1988) 'Death Row Dilemma' *National Law Journal* 35.

Kipling (1940), 'The Old Issue', *Rudyard Kipling's Verse*, Definitive Edition, London.

Kronman, Anthony T. (1987), 'A Life in the Law', *University of Chicago Law Review*, vol. 54, pp. 835-876.

Law Reform Commission of Victoria (July 1991), 'Access to the law: Accountability of the legal profession', *Discussion Paper* no. 24, pp. 16-23

Luban, D. (1988), *Lawyers and Justice*, Princeton University Press.

Macaulay (1914), *Essay on Bacon*, Solomon, (ed.), London.

Melbourne Punch (15 July 1886).

New South Wales Law Reform Commission (May 1992), 'Three Options for Regulatory Reform' in *Scrutiny of the Legal Profession: Complaints Against Lawyers*, Discussion Paper, Chapter 5, pp. 169-175.

Phillips, Alfred (1990), *Professional Ethics for Scottish Solicitors*, Butterworth.

Plato, *Theaetetus* (172 173) John McDowell trs., (1973), Clarendon Press, Oxford.

Postema, Gerald (1986), 'Moral Responsibility in Professional Ethics in Davis and Elliston, eds., *Ethics and the Legal Profession*, Prometheus Books, New York.

Tur, Richard H.S. (1992) vol. 1, pp. 73-97 'Confidentiality and Account- ability, *Griffith Law Review* , 73-97

Tur, Richard H.S. (1993), 'An Introduction to Lawyers' Ethics' *Journal of Professional Legal Education*, July.

White, James Boyd (1985), *Heracles Bow: Essays on the Rhetorics and Poetics of Law*, pp. 49-59.

6 Accountability and nursing

Win Tadd

Introduction

Accountability is viewed as the sine qua non of any professional group, and much has been written on this topic in relation to the nurse.[1] Most dictionary definitions of the term emphasize answerability for one's actions and suggest that it is synonymous with responsibility. Before trying to answer questions such as 'To whom is the nurse accountable?' and 'For what is the nurse accountable?' therefore, it may be helpful to spend some time considering 'responsibility' which some authors see as being a wider concept. In adopting this approach it is hoped that some of the confusion which exists in the minds of individual nurses in relation to accountability will be removed or reduced. Also, and perhaps more importantly, it is hoped to show that in considerations of accountability, the emphasis on the individual, which is the position adopted by nursing's statutory body, represents an inadequate standpoint. This inadequacy does not simply relate to conceptual clarity but also to principles of justice and fairness, as it may help to avoid the invidious position of nurses being unreasonably 'called to account' when in fact responsibility for the state of affairs lies elsewhere.

Responsibility

The terms 'responsible' and 'responsibility' are commonly used in a variety of ways. First, responsibility is frequently a result of a role which one adopts. In this sense it might be said that as a parent, one has a duty or is responsible for the way in which one cares for one's children. Here, the term responsibility is synonymous with duty, but it is worthwhile highlighting that a duty or responsibility can be assigned by another individual or group, or it can be assumed voluntarily. In considerations of professional duty or responsibility, it is again worth emphasizing that an individual invariably chooses to enter a profession, unlike being born into a particular family or religion (Muyskens, 1982, p. 163).

Second, the term responsibility is often used to indicate a causal relationship with a particular event or outcome. For example, 'Jane is responsible for the dent in the car', meaning that she was involved in some incident with the car.

Finally, the term responsibility is used in an evaluative sense to indicate blame or culpability and this often follows an assessment of an individual's responsibility in one of the first two senses. Someone who fails to fulfil a duty or responsibility associated with a particular role may be held responsible; similarly someone who is causally responsible for an adverse consequence may be subject to blame or punishment.

Clearly, responsibility is a complex concept whose main features include accountability, liability, rationality and the absence of negligence (Agich, 1982, p. 55). Accountability is a requirement of the first two uses of the term, be it in relation to a role such as parent or nurse; or for a particular action, but as Agich says, to describe an agent as accountable certain conditions must be met. These include an understanding of the required conduct or actions in particular situations; the ability and autonomy to make judgements about alternative actions or decisions; and the capacity to give reasons as to why one chose to act in a particular way. Without this being case, it is difficult to describe a person as being responsible or to allocate accountability.

Agich suggests that the complicated nature of the philosophical literature on responsibility is in part due to the fact that one or other of these features described above assumes particular importance in particular cases. However another reason which might account for the complexity when dealing with issues of responsibility is the way in which certain elements are concerned with the agent's character, abilities and personality, such as the willingness to consider possible actions rationally and to exercise care so that harmful consequences can be avoided, whilst others, namely accountability and liability must viewed within the context of the prevailing social and institutional conditions. For example, the fact that Mary was driving the car when the dent was sustained, does not mean that she is accountable. It may be that a third party drove into the back of her vehicle, or dropped a brick onto the bonnet. In both cases it would be unfair to hold Mary accountable.

Before leaving responsibility it is important to draw another distinction which will be pertinent to the discussion of accountability which follows. This distinction involves the notions of 'task responsibility' and 'role responsibility' (Agich, 1982, pp. 65-8). Task responsibility was defined by Ladd (1975, pp. 98-125) as being institutionally determined, as an aspect of particular positions or jobs held within an organization. Because the nature of this type of responsibility is determined by the superior subordinate relationships which exist within a particular institution, task responsibility is limited, and can be delegated, constructed and terminated, according to the commands of the superior who allocates it. Thus notions of authority and authorization come into play. Task responsibility is therefore owed to the person or the institution from which the authorization to act flows. Further, task responsibility requires very little in the way of deliberation, critical reflection and judgement demanding only that the individual agent avoids negligent action (Agich, 1982, p. 67).

Role responsibility on the other hand is attached to social roles and the significant and socially valued relationships which they entail. As such it is diffuse and indeterminate as it exists to achieve certain ends or broad aims as for instance, the role of parent involves a host of aims which are relative to the wellbeing of children. Some of these may be short term or immediate such as providing food and clothing and may well include specific tasks, but others are broader and longer term and involve a consideration of the prevailing 'sociomoral norms' which provide both justifications and constraints in relation to the particular roles and the ends which they serve (Agich, 1982, p. 65).

Clearly therefore, in considerations of role responsibility, it is necessary to undertake analysis at different levels from that of individual action. In particular, one cannot ignore the institutional and social contexts within which a particular role is enacted, as the distribution of power and authority, which is a direct result of these factors, assumes great importance in determining how individuals will be called to account in everyday practical terms. Another important feature of role responsibility, because of its nonspecific nature, is that the individual must exercise considerable deliberation and discretion in the exercise of her duties. Further, this type of responsibility is typically owed to the recipient of the service being offered. Bearing these distinctions in mind it is now appropriate to consider the nature of accountability in nursing.

Accountability in nursing

Rhodes (1983, pp. 65-6) suggests that answers to questions about the nurse's accountability will depend upon the particular ideological stance which an individual adopts. He goes on to outline three dominant ideologies which prevail within health care settings.

Bureaucratic ideology

Within this model, the nurse is viewed as a servant of the institution and as such, she draws her authority to act from the organization itself through the hierarchy of superior-subordinate relationships. In fulfilling her various duties, she must comply with institutional policies and regulations and her accountability for the performance of these delegated functions is to the individuals who occupy senior positions within the institution. Providing that she acts in accordance with the established rules and policies, the institution will accept some degree of the nurse's accountability to law, in the form of vicarious liability, whenever there is a question of litigation or complaint. This reflects the position which Feinberg (1970, pp. 226-7) called the 'bound agent' as in the eyes of the law, the institution and the nurse stand in a 'master-servant relationship' (Rhodes, 1983, p. 65) and therefore the master is held partially accountable for the actions of the servant.

This ideology has always been particularly prominent within nursing with its traditional emphasis on obedience and loyalty to the employing institution (Winslow, 1984), and there is no doubt that many nurses gain a certain amount of comfort and security from being able to hide behind the idea that providing they follow their superior's orders they are safe from personal criticism (Copp and Boylan, 1992, pp. 42-3). Since the introduction of general management and the increasing number of hospitals opting for independent trust status, it is likely that this bureaucratic ideology will enjoy increasing prominence.

Paramedical ideology

A second ideology put forward is that of 'paramedical ideology' (Rhodes, 1983, pp. 65-6). On this account, nursing is viewed as being subordinate to medicine which provides authorization in accordance with agreed protocols for the implementation of prescribed treatments. The nurse is thus accountable to the doctor for carrying out his prescriptions, for which he retains ultimate authority. Although this view has always been a dominant one,[2] additional force was given to it in 1977 when the then Department of Health and Social Security (DHSS, 1977) published a circular in relation to the extended role of the nurse. This extension involved certain nurses taking on additional tasks usually performed by doctors, such as administering intravenous injections or undertaking defibrillation when a patient suffered a cardiac arrest. To undertake these functions however, the nurse had to undergo specific training and was invariably awarded a certificate of competence signed by an appropriate medical officer. Again the nurse was afforded some protection in law as

91

the task remained the responsibility of the doctor, but could be delegated to those nurses who had acquired the competence to fulfil them.

Although there were some positive effects of this for patients, the main beneficiary was undoubtedly the doctor who, for example, did not have to be called to the ward at an unsociable hour to give an intravenous injection of an antibiotic. The fact that the patient's interests were of a secondary nature is evidenced by the fact that the nurse could not use her new skill and her discretion to give a patient an intravenous injection of a pain killing drug, even if this was prescribed by the doctor to be given when necessary, or at least not without first checking with the doctor. With the recent reductions in junior doctor's hours, it is expected that there will be a significant increase in the numbers of traditionally regarded medical tasks being delegated to nursing staff.

Professional ideology

The third perspective reflects an ideology of professionalism (Rhodes, 1983, p. 66) in which the nurse is viewed as an independent agent contracted to provide a specialist service and owing allegiance and a duty of care directly to the patient or client. On this view, the authority to act stems directly from the individual's knowledge and competence and accountability is owed for the services which one is contracted to provide. From this perspective, the nurse owes accountability across a broad spectrum: first and foremost it is to the patient; next to society generally, especially as members of professions are accorded special privileges and status; and finally to the profession of nursing whose standards she is expected to uphold. Within this view, accountability is for the total service and it is much more difficult to isolate where it begins and ends as the nurse is expected to make professional judgements and use her discretion in determining how nursing care can best be organized and delivered.

The problem for the nurse in relation to these differing ideologies, is that there is an assumption that they can coexist. Hospital managers and doctors for example (and some nurses themselves) view nursing from the first two perspectives, while nursing's professional bodies assert that it is the third perspective which is to be adopted.

If we now return to the accounts of task and role responsibility described above, it will be evident why these ideologies are incompatible. The first two positions reflect task responsibility, with accountability corresponding to answerability limited to the tasks which have been undertaken, be they delegated by a senior officer of the institution or the doctor. The ideology of professionalism however, reflects role responsibility and accountability is therefore much more diffuse and broad based. The conflict arises because the particular type of responsibility

92

which an individual shoulders is to a large extent a reflection of the amount of autonomy and control which they exercise in relation to their work.

Task responsibility for example, is associated with an individual only being allowed to act within strict limits set by whoever delegates or creates the particular task. Thus although a nurse might be expected to give an injection or complete a procedure according to previously agreed protocols or policies, she is not expected to exercise discretion in relation to the dosage, timing or perhaps even withholding of the treatment.

In relation to role responsibility however, the degree of autonomy exercised by the individual occupant of the role is considerable. In this case, an individual is employed because of her expertise in supplying a service, and she is expected to demonstrate discretion and judgement in determining how that service can best be provided. Thus accountability takes on a much wider brief in relation to the execution of the duties. Viewed in this capacity, nurses, employed to provide a nursing service, would be accountable for any decision making and delegation involved in the control and organization of nursing work. Who might perform particular nursing tasks, how they would be organized, as well as determining the nature of nursing work, would all be part of this remit.

Whilst this situation of different and conflicting expectations for nurses remains, the position of the individual nurse is doubtful and open to abuse and it is vital therefore that the position of nursing's statutory body is considered. Especially as an important function of the Council is to sometimes 'call in the dues' owed in the name of accountability by insisting that individual nurses appear in front of the Professional Conduct Committee where they are required to give an account of their actions, whenever misconduct or malpractice is alleged.

The UKCC and accountability

The UKCC publications, the *Code of Professional Conduct* (UKCC, 1992) and the advisory document, *Exercising Accountability* (UKCC, 1989) reflect the standpoint of a professional ideology. The *Code of Professional Conduct* emphasizes that every nurse, midwife and health visitor is personally accountable for his or her practice and in the exercise of professional accountability must uphold each of the sixteen clauses of the Code. The advisory document adds to this general expectation of accountability on the part of each registered nurse by providing specific information in relation to five key aspects of the nurse's role. The key aspects are:

1. Concern in respect of the environment of care.
2. Consent and truth.
3. Advocacy on behalf of patients and clients.
4. Collaboration and co-operation in care.
5. Objection to participation in care and treatment

Although within the confines of this paper it will not be possible to undertake a detailed analysis of each of these key aspects, an examination of the first should demonstrate that insufficient consideration has been given to what is actually being asked of nurses in relation to their accountability for nursing services.

The requirement for concern in respect of the environment of care demands that all registered nurses:

> make appropriate representations about the environment of care (a) where patients or clients seem likely to be placed in jeopardy and/or standards of practice endangered; (b) where the staff in such settings are at risk because of the pressure of work and/or inadequacy of resources (which again place patients at risk; and (c) where valuable resources are being used inappropriately (UKCC, 1989, p. 8).

As highlighted previously, the nature of role responsibility demands that attention is paid not only to the actions of individual agents, but also to the institutional and social settings in which a role is enacted and yet little attention appears to have been paid by the UKCC to the rapidly changing culture, or to the realities of the political climate in which today's health care is delivered.

The introduction of the general management following the report of a management inquiry team appointed to investigate ways of improving the cost-effectiveness and efficiency of the National Health Service (Griffiths, 1983) has had far-reaching effects on both the environment of care and the likelihood of staff speaking out. In addition, the business principles and market place values that have been increasingly introduced into health and social service settings by the publication of the White Papers, *Working for Patients* (Department of Health, 1989a) and its eight working papers and *Community Care in the Next Decade and Beyond* (Department of Health, 1989b) have further subjected the provision of health care to stringent budgetary control and regulation and overall reductions in public sector spending. When strategies such as these are coupled with a social climate of high unemployment they amount to a significant controlling force which should not be ignored.

One result of these changes has been the constraint placed on health care professionals, especially nurses, as the autonomy required to interpret their role and respond to particular needs has been seriously circumscribed by the requirements placed on them by professional managers. Whilst agreeing that it is incumbent on all professionals to ensure that their expertise and skills are used to the best advantage and not wasted, there is a danger that in relentlessly attempting to reduce a role to its constituent tasks, significant and socially valued aspects may be lost. For example, when nurses try to dissect nursing practice, with all of its various facets, into the measurable categories demanded by nurse workload systems, they quickly discover that there is no formal or managerial vocabulary to express the emotive, intuitive or creative dimensions of their work. These elements of nursing work although often essential to the recipients of care, have largely remained invisible and have therefore been eliminated from, or disregarded by studies of workload. In other words, nursing may have Gestalt-like qualities in that the role entails more than the performance of its constituent tasks.

It is of course very difficult for any professional worker to argue against such initiatives from this standpoint, as almost immediately one is charged with adopting a position of self-protection. Yet the tendency for job analysis to result in deskilling and deprofessionalisation is well recognized and occurs when the breaking down of an occupation's knowledge and skills into its component parts results in the worker being 'divorced from the totality of the labour process' and denied autonomy of action (Robinson, 1991, p. 295) which is essential for accountability within the context of a social role.

The adoption of reductionist approaches, such as measures of patient dependence or nurse workload, when used solely to reduce costs invariably results in 'less effective levels of care' and the 'deskilling of nurses because the craft and creativity of nursing is destroyed' (Storch and Stinson, 1988, p. 36). This deprofessionalisation expands as professionals increasingly find themselves working as subordinate employees within centralized bureaucracies and although it might be argued that this has always been the case in hospital nursing, it has been suggested (Storch and Stinson, 1988, p. 37) that this process may have further to go.

When a task such as the care of a particular patient is divided into its isolated parts, then knowledge of the total assignment is lost as the individual parts may even be allocated to different types of workers. To some extent this has already happened with increasing numbers of health care support workers being employed to undertake certain elements of patient care. Nurses in such a situation may no longer have control over the way in which the role of these ancillary workers is defined or performed, so that eventually influence over the social purpose of nursing work is lost (Storch and Stinson, 1988).

It is not only the managerial climate within the institution that is of relevance however, attention must also be paid to the prevailing economic and political climate. Nurses and health care staff, like the general population, are susceptible to the daily messages in the media and soon begin to believe that economic stringency is necessary for the nation's wealth, especially as everyday they see the realities of limited resources. Challenge is seen to be of no avail as there appears to be no credible alternative to the view that the welfare budget is not a bottomless pit.

Thus the prevailing political and social ideology assumes an authority which shapes people's responses, their actions and to a certain extent, their autonomy. As far as nurses are concerned, they are much less likely to speak out when they cannot easily find alternative employment and so they are increasingly affected by opposing tensions which appear to grow daily — for instance, the tension between the emphasis on rules and conformity within the employing institution and the demands for professional accountability and responsibility as espoused by the UKCC.

There is also a tension between the demands of an increasing workload and the ever growing complexity of tasks and the limited time, staffing, and resources available to achieve them. Even where grievances are justified, a climate of rigorous budgetary control and cuts in services allows management to argue the impossibility of fulfilling such demands or resolving the problems. If staff continue to complain then a common rebuttal is that they are irresponsible and unreasonable. Graham Pink's experience is a typical case in point where attempts to discredit him as being unrealistic, unreasonable and hysterical were repeatedly made by his immediate superiors and the hospital's management team (Turner, 1992, pp. 26-8).

The consequences of this for accountability should be readily apparent. In such a climate, questioning and debate do not figure largely in the ideology of 'good management' pursued by general managers. Dissenters tend to be quickly and resolutely dealt with and the most important institutional mission appears to be to do more with less. The increase in numbers of managers by eighty per cent since 1987 (*Nursing Times*, 1993, p. 6) has emphasized and intensified this top-down, centre-periphery model of management with its associated bureaucratic ideology within the health service (Hunter, 1990).

Thus for the nurse there are conflicts not only in relation to conflicting ideologies concerning her role and responsibilities within the health care setting, but there also exist powerful external ideologies which (even if she were willing and eager to accept role responsibility with its attendant requirements for her accountability) impinge on her ability to actually do so.

In the type of scenario described above, the nurse's role is reduced to one in which she has little or no control over the delivery of nursing services generally. Other than paying attention to the individual qualities which she brings to her role, such as compassion and an acceptance of the importance of respect and dignity for the patient, she can do little to influence the nature of nursing as she lacks the necessary power and ability. Graham Pink[3] for instance suggests that his role was reduced to one of virtual custodian, rather than nurse, because of the impoverished and inadequate resources he had at his disposal.

Each of the key aspects of the UKCC's advisory document could be analysed in a similar manner and found wanting in terms of the practical realities of the nurse's accountability. For example, 'consent and truth' and 'advocacy on behalf of patients and clients' are unlikely to flourish within an environment such as the one which currently prevails. This is evidenced by what are referred to as 'gagging clauses' in new contracts of employment issued by NHS Trusts and the Government's *Guidance for Staff on Relations with the Public and the Media* (NHS Directorate, 1993) offers little in the way of reassurance or clarity for staff who, having raised concerns about standards, remain dissatisfied by any management action taken.

Similarly 'collaboration and cooperation in care' are soon replaced by conspiracy and coercion when autonomy is so limited. Likewise, 'objection to participation in care and treatment' is less of a viable option when individuals become increasingly afraid for their own jobs and future security in a constraining climate of competition and control. Instead the fainthearted are more likely to review their principles and undertake personally distasteful tasks, despite the consequences for their self-respect and personal morality.

There is however little indication that the UKCC is willing to reconsider their position in relation to the nurse's accountability. Recently, for example, Reg Pyne (1992), UKCC Assistant Registrar for Standards and Ethics, suggested that accountability and empowerment are inextricably linked, in that empowerment is derived from accountability. He makes this claim on a number of grounds which pertain to the Code of Professional Conduct. Those relevant to this discussion are that first, the code holds each nurse accountable for her actions and thus as she knows exactly where she stands and what is expected of her, she is empowered; second, because of the emphasis which the code places on the nurse's fundamental obligation to promote and act in the patient's interest the nurse is empowered as she is able to show the code to those who doubt the nurse's value; third, he claims that to be able to 'stand up and be counted' with support from the statutory body is empowering; fourth, by encouraging nurses to speak out when all is not well Pyne claims that the code promotes 'truth over pretence' and when a number of people choose truth, this is empowering.

There is much to be challenged amongst Pyne's claims. For example, nurses, both singly and collectively, might show a greater inclination to speak out, if the UKCC was seen to condemn the conditions under which not only the majority of nurses are expected to work, but also patient care is delivered. Also, the UKCC could do much to clarify the status and standing of the code in relation to both contracts of employment and the law, so that nurses acting in good faith are not unfairly penalized.

However the major challenge which this paper will make is to the claim that because every nurse is aware of the expectations placed on her in relation to professional accountability, she is therefore empowered. Rather than finding this empowering, some individuals may argue that this is in fact extremely costly to the individual concerned. Graham Pink is one such nurse who has expressed serious reservations about the value of the code (Cole, 1991). In today's climate, a demanding code could prove an additional burden which simply causes nurses to feel less powerful and more guilty.

As Tadd (1991) points out, without appropriate support systems in place for those nurses who are sufficiently concerned about poor practice that they make their complaints official, then it could be argued that unrealistic demands are being placed on individual nurses. He goes on to suggest that if the statutory body is aware of the personal consequences facing nurses who adhere to the demands of code and in spite of this, it continues to demand such adherence, then its own ethical standards are suspect and deserve critical examination.

Tadd also makes the point that nurses, like other people, may have a variety of competing demands made upon them and it is not always possible to keep these separate.

Most nurses are happy in the job of providing care to those in need, but they have to work in order to feed themselves and their own families. These duties are in addition to those to patients. If they forfeit their chances of making progress in their careers by whistleblowing activities, they could be charged with acting unethically towards their own dependants. Thus the mere assertion that because an individual is aware of the demands and expectations placed upon them, she is empowered, can be challenged. If the demands and expectations are too excessive then they can be seen as oppressive rather than empowering, especially when there is a lack of support.

The whole problem with the way that Pyne discusses accountability is that he speaks of it within the context of a professional ideology so that it involves an acceptance of role responsibility, and as such, it is a limitless requirement. Adopting this stance means that once a nurse is qualified, then she is accountable for everything which occurs in her immediate vicinity, for every aspect of client care, but this is to ignore the interplay of social and institutional forces.

No fudging, no uncertainty, no ambiguity to be found there. You are personally accountable for your practice. In other words noone else, be they medical practitioner, more senior colleague, manager or whosoever else can bear your accountability for you. It is all down to you (Pyne, 1992, p. 5). Such a view of accountability, which focuses solely on the individual and denies any collective responsibility for the prevailing state of affairs, rather than being empowering is in fact the reverse, as placing unrealistic demands on people tends to result in feelings of guilt which are disempowering and damaging to the individual's self-esteem.

As Agich (1982) showed, one can only fairly be held accountable for those aspects of care, or the care environment, over which one can exercise control and it is this illusion that an individual is either accountable or not accountable that must be corrected. Failure to do so means that we are always in danger of committing the either/or fallacy, by not recognizing that there may be many aspects of client care for which the nurse is not accountable, because she does not have the power or authority to influence the aspect under consideration.

Perhaps the claim that the notions of accountability are empowering would be more meaningful if the UKCC undertook a critical appraisal of what responsibility means in practice and established different standards or levels to be maintained by individual nurses working in varying positions of authority. So that, for example, nurse managers would be accountable for ensuring the availability of resources to meet patient's and student's needs; registered nurses would be accountable for their knowledge and competency in relation to the delivery of client care, and nurse educators would be held accountable for the standards of education offered to nursing students.

This action is particularly important in clinical practice as nursing care has traditionally been delivered by a number of individuals all prepared to varying degrees of competence, but who each use the title nurse in some way. For example the registered nurse may have been trained through a three year educational programme, she may have been prepared by an undergraduate degree in nursing, she may have undertaken further education in the form of advanced clinical courses, a master's or even a doctoral degree. She may on the other hand have undertaken a two year course of preparation which will enable registration as a second level practitioner. Added to this there are student nurses at various stages of their educational programme and nursing auxiliaries who are largely untrained.

Although it might be argued that there should be significant differences in the level of nursing activities undertaken by each of these different groups, this is not always the case, especially when staffing levels are low and the demand for nursing care is high. It is certainly far from easy to appreciate the differences in preparation and therefore the abilities, of such a wide range of individuals and as a result, role ambiguity not only in relation to practice, but also in relation to the scope of responsibility and accountability is high.

The UKCC as the profession's statutory body, must therefore take some responsibility for failing to achieve role clarity and for not identifying the rightful domain of the different categories of nurse. If such an analysis were undertaken then it might be possible to discriminate between practitioners and thereby link the degree of accountability to the level of knowledge and expertise, and to the amount of power and authority held by individual nurses. Because the UKCC attempts to set a single standard of accountability without recognising that 'nursing' covers a wide range of occupational categories, it fails to discriminate where there are relevant differences.

Care must be taken to avoid giving the impression that the nurse should be excused all accountability or responsibility, as there are some distinct areas in which nurses do have both power and authority. Consequently it is reasonable that, in these particular areas, they should be held to account. But the concept of professional accountability as it is currently portrayed has been inflated to such a degree that it has been made to extend to each and every part of the nursing role. It disregards the fact that whilst a practitioner may have autonomy in relation to some aspects of her work, this does not of itself signify that she is fully autonomous. Just as there are degrees of autonomy, so there are degrees of accountability and this is what the UKCC fails to recognise.

Not everyone is of the same opinion however. Geoff Hunt (1992) takes a rather harsh line and suggests that where reality and professional expectations clash, it should be reality which is changed. He goes on to ask:

> What if the code-makers were to say to themselves: "Well it is difficult for nurses to be fair, honest, conscientious and caring so we won't ask them to be" (Hunt, 1992, p. 21).

One must not be misled by such clever sophistry, for the alternative is not to suggest that nurses should not shoulder any measure of accountability, but simply that a more balanced and reasonable view should be taken of the expectations that a nurse might be expected to fulfil.

The concern raised here, is that the standard of accountability placed upon nurses, in the absence of any adequate support network or recognition of external factors, is unreasonable.

> unreasonable because they proclaim the registered nurse to be an
> accountable professional yet fail to acknowledge that in the real world
> of modern health care, very little power is invested in the world of the
> bedside nurse (Tadd, 1993).

Accountability implies that the individual can decide not only on various aspects of an act, such as for instance, its worthiness but also that she has a range of options open to her — for example, that she can refuse to undertake the act, or that it is in her power to decide precisely how a particular act will be performed. If such choices are not available, or they are so restricted as to be meaningless, then it is difficult to see how individuals can be held to account (Tadd, 1993).

It seems reasonable to expect therefore that the UKCC recognize the potential for conflict in relation to accountability and rather than merely continuing to exhort the concept of professional accountability, undertake a critical appraisal of what its demands mean in everyday practical terms. A continued failure to do this means that rather than an empowering force, professional accountability will remain a stick with which individual nurses are repeatedly beaten, whilst the system and its supporters are condoned.

Notes

1. See for example, Clifford, J.C. (1981), 'Managerial Control Versus
    Professional Accountability: A Paradox', *Journal of Nursing Adminis-
    tration* , vol. 11, no. 9, pp. 19 -21; Copp, G.(1988), 'Professional
    Accountability: The Conflict', *Nursing Times,* vol. 84, no. 43, pp. 42-4;
    Hyde, P. (1985), 'Management: Accountability', *Nursing Mirror,* vol. 3,
    no. 16, pp. 17-8; Jackson, A. (1983), 'Accountability in Nursing: The
    Practitioner's View', *Nursing Times,* vol. 79, no. 36, pp. 67-8; Lewis, F
    and Batey, M. (1982), 'Clarifying Autonomy and Accountability in
    Nursing Service', Parts 1 and 2, *Journal of Nursing Administration,*
    vol.12, pp. 13-8; Mauksch, H. (1966), 'The Organisational Context of
    Nursing Practice' in Davis, F. (ed.), *The Nursing Profession: Five
    Sociological Essays,* John Wiley & Sons, New York; McFarlane, J.
    Baroness (1980), 'Accountability in Nursing' in *Accountability in
    Nursing: The Report of a Seminar for Fellows of the Royal College of
    Nursing,* RCN., London; Mundinger, M. (1980), *Autonomy in Nursing,*
    Aspen Co., New Jersey; Rhodes, B. (1983), 'Accountability in Nursing:
    Alternative Perspectives', *Nursing Times,* September 7, pp. 65-6; Rye,

D.(1982), 'Accountability in Nursing', *Nursing Focus*, April, pp. 90-2; Singleton, E. and Nail, F. (1984), 'Autonomy in Nursing', *Nursing Forum*, vol. XXI, no. 3, pp. 123-30; Singleton, E. and Nail, F. (1984), 'Role Clarification: A Pre-requisite for Autonomy', *Journal of Nursing Administration*, vol. 11, no. 9, pp.19-21; Styles, M. (1985), 'Accountable to Whom?', *International Nursing Review*, vol. 32, no.3, pp. 73-5.

2. See for example, Jameton, A. (1984), *Nursing Practice: The Ethical Issues*, Prentice-Hall, Englewood-Cliffs, N.J. Chapter 3 in particular demonstrates the prevalence of these attitudes.

3. Personal communication.

References

Agich, G.J. (1982), 'Concepts of responsibility in medicine', in Agich, G.J.(ed.), *Responsibility in Medicine*, Reidel, Dordrecht.

Cole, A. (1991), 'Upholding the Code', *Nursing Times*, vol. 87, no. 27, pp. 26-9.

Department of Health (1989a), *Working for Patients: the Health Service - Caring for the 1990s* , HMSO, London.

Department of Health (1989b), *Caring for People: Community Care in the Next Decade and Beyond*, HMSO, London.

Department of Health and Social Security (DHSS) (1977), 'The extended role of the nurse', HMSO, London.

Feinberg, J. (1970), *Doing and Deserving: Essays in the Theory of Responsibility*, Princeton University Press, Princeton.

Griffiths, R. (1983), *Report on the National Health Service Management Inquiry*, Department of Health and Social Services, London.

Hunt, G. (1992), 'News focus', *Nursing Times* 88, vol. 25, pp.21-2.

Hunter, D.J. (1990), 'Managing the cracks: management development for healthcare interfaces', *Journal of Health Planning and Management*, vol. 5, pp. 7-14.

Ladd, J. (1975), 'The ethics of participation' in Pennock, J.R. and Chapman, J. (eds.), *Participation in Politics: Nomos* XVI, Lieber-Atherton, New York, pp. 98-125.

Muyskens, J.L. (1982), *Moral Problems in Nursing: A Philosophical Investigation*, Rowman and Littlefield, Totowa, N.J.

NHS Directorate, Welsh Office (1993), *Guidance for Staff on Relations with the Public and the Media*, NHS Directorate, Cardiff.

Pyne, R. (1992) 'Empowerment through using the Code of Professional Conduct', paper presented at conference on Use and Abuse of Power, Queen Margaret College, Edinburgh, 15 September.

Rhodes, B. (1983), 'Accountability in nursing: alternative perspectives', *Nursing Times*, 7 September, pp. 65-6.

Robinson, J. (1991), 'Power, politics and policy analysis in nursing' in Perry, A. and Jolley, M. (eds), *Nursing: A Knowledge Base for Practice*, Edward Arnold, London.

Storch, J.L. and Stinson, S.M. (1988), 'Concepts of deprofessional-isation with application to nursing', in White, (ed.), *Political Issues in Nursing: Past, Present and Future*, vol. 3, John Wiley, Chichester.

Tadd, G.V. (1991), 'Where are the whistle-blowers?', *Nursing Times*, vol. 87 no. 1, pp.42-4.

Tadd, G.V. (1994) 'Professional codes: an exercise in tokenism', *Nursing Ethics*, vo. 1, no. 1.

Turner, T. (1992), 'The Indomitable Mr. Pink', *Nursing Times*, vol. 88, no. 24, pp. 26-8.

United Kingdom Central Council for Nursing, Midwifery and Health Visiting (1992), *Code of Professional Conduct* , 3rd edn, UKCC, London.

United Kingdom Central Council for Nursing, Midwifery and Health Visiting (1989), *Exercising Accountability: A Framework to Assist Nurses, Midwives and Health Visitors to Consider Ethical Aspects of Professional Practice*, UKCC, London.

Winslow, G.R. (1984), 'From loyalty to advocacy', *Hastings Center Report*, June, pp. 32-40.

7 Professional codes and Kantian duties

Nigel G. E. Harris

A professional body may introduce a code of conduct for one or more of several different reasons. Doing so may be viewed as a useful public relations exercise which will enhance the profession's status. Where the professional body has been criticized for failing to control the actions of maverick members it may help counter those seeking to have self-regulation replaced by statutory control. Having a code can assist members to defend themselves against clients, particularly in litigation where malpractice is claimed, by delimiting responsibilities. But these and some other possible uses to which codes may be put are not their purported ones. It would be a rash professional body which dared to admit publicly that these were the only or even the main reasons for having a code. Taken at face value a code presents a set of principles of action to which it is desirable that members of the profession should conform.

There are two ways in which prescribed professional behaviour may be desirable. Many codes contain clauses which set out a preferred method of carrying out some task. In many professional situations it is advantageous to have standardized procedures, since this will improve efficiency, yet the choice of standard taken may be arbitrary. Codes which consist largely or entirely of such clauses — what I shall refer to as 'standardizing clauses' — are often called codes of practice. There are, however, many professional codes which contain clauses which are not aimed at achieving standardization, but purport to have more direct ethical force. They say do this or do that, not because it is good to have everyone do things the same way, but because this is how one ought to act if one is to act ethically.

Now either the apparent moral content of these 'ethical' clauses is just a sham, or it really is something that can be taken as giving them status as moral precepts. If the clauses of a code are thought of as having

104

genuine ethical content then a question has to be faced, namely, what is the basis for that content? In traditional thinking about ethics principles of the level of generality found in codes of conduct are not self-justifying, but need to be seen as applied principles of some general moral theory. But what moral theory could be taken as backing these claims?

I shall start by showing that given their terminology, the matters covered by them, and the situations in which appeal is made to them, 'ethical' clauses from codes appear to fit most easily into a deontological moral theory of the Kantian kind. I shall argue that they are more easily reconciled with a Kantian ethics than with alternative theories. However, I shall then show that even trying to provide a deontological basis raises problems. Why these problems are serious is that they bring into question whether the principles set out in the codes can rightly be treated as ethical at all.

Why a Kantian interpretation is the most plausible

A check I made through the codes of nearly 150 professions in Britain[1] showed that all consisted of a series of clauses expressed as imperatives or as what members have undertaken to do. Two-thirds said that members 'shall' do certain things and 'shall not' do others. Other expressions frequently used in this context are: 'must', 'should', 'are obliged to', 'undertake to', 'agree to'.

Some typical clauses are:

A member shall perform only those services which are within the member's competence (Harris, 1989, p. 168).

A member shall at all times uphold the principle that equal consideration should be given to all regardless of gender, marital status, sexual orientation, creed, colour, race or ethnic origin, religion, disablement or nationality (Harris, 1989, p. 219).

A member *shall* at all times take care to avoid waste of natural resources, damage to the environment, and damage or destruction of the products of human skill and industry (*The Production Engineer*, 1975, p. 2).

Similar clauses to each of these are found in many other codes.

These and most other clauses from codes are categorical rather than hypothetical imperatives. They say of actions of some type that they are what ought to be done, but they do not say do this, or do not do this, because such-and-such will result. From their linguistic structure they conform to the Kantian idea of the sorts of moral rule we should take to govern our actions.

Of course, this does not imply that those who adopt a code must have a Kantian ethics. Any moral theory can be expressed in imperatives or using deontological terminology. For example, a utilitarian could say we all have a duty to promote the greatest general happiness. But when we try to formulate more specific rules of action, then the utilitarian has to claim that we have a duty, say, to refrain from lying except in limited circumstances, because of its felicific benefits. At the level of specificity about actions found in codes of conduct, the consequentialist would have to adopt hypothetical, not categorical, imperatives.

It is not that clauses from codes never mention consequences. For instance, damage to the environment could result from some of the actions production engineers might carry out, and their code requires them to take all reasonable steps to avoid it. An unharmed environment is something for which an engineer may strive, yet in the Institution of Production Engineers' code it is not treated as an ultimate end, but rather — in the Kantian way — as something a rational will could happily envisage being effected by all actions, and so a possible basis for a principle of action.

It might be objected that it is wrong to reject a consequentialist basis for the principles in codes on the grounds that the principles themselves do not require individual justification. Rather, we should seek a justification only for a code as a whole, and that justification can be found in the benefits from increased efficiency and cooperation that result from the adoption of a code. This view has been argued for by Michael Davis, who writes:

> . . a profession is a group of persons who want to cooperate in serving the same ideal better than they could if they did not cooperate. Engineers, for example, might be thought to serve the ideal of efficient design, construction, and maintenance of safe and useful objects. A code of ethics would then prescribe how professionals are to pursue their common ideal so that each may do the best she can at minimal cost to herself and those she cares about (including the public, if looking after the public is part of what she cares about). The code is to protect each professional from certain pressures (for example, the pressure to cut corners to save money) by making it reasonably likely (and more likely than otherwise) that most other

members of the profession will *not* take advantage of her good conduct. A code protects members of a profession from certain consequences of competition. A code is a solution to a coordination problem (Davis, 1991, p.2).

One of the more obvious troubles with this account is that it makes it hard to explain why so much space in codes is devoted to the protection of clients, since many of these safeguards will not decrease competition between members of the profession. Another is that the notion of 'ideal' used is extremely wide. The engineers who designed the ovens at Auschwitz used to cremate Holocaust victims could well have claimed that they conformed to it (the ovens being safe to those operating them and useful for disposing of corpses, whatever their source). Efficiency and cooperative endeavour may serve the public good, but in some cases they may do the opposite. Suppose, for instance, drug dealers came together and drew up a code of conduct which, if followed, would enable them to ply their trade more effectively. This would hardly make their trade more ethical.

Davis is not unaware of this problem. He asks:

What if most engineers were moral monsters or just self-serving opportunists? What then? Interpreting their codes would certainly be different, and probably harder. We could not understand it as a *professional* code. We would have to switch to principles of interpretation we reserve for mere folkways, Nazi statues, or the like. We would have to leave the presuppositions of ethics behind (Davis, 1991, pp. 163-4).

Davis sees the place where ethics comes into professional codes as being with their authorship. Those who draw up a genuinely professional code must be doing so within a presupposed ethical framework, and so would not author a code that 'would include anything people generally considered immoral, (Davis, 1991, p.163). This may deal with my case of the drugs dealer, but not with the Auschwitz oven designers. A rule which helps to improve efficiency and whose authors rightly envisage will in general be beneficial would not be thought of as an immoral rule, yet there may be circumstances in which someone with immoral intentions who follows the rule will thereby achieve greater evil.

Davis's account categorizes all the principles within codes as standardizing clauses. For such a clause there may well be the indirect consequentialist justification which proceeds as follows:

1. General adherence to this clause increases efficiency or cooperation;
2. Efficiency or cooperation enables the profession in question to do more work;
3. The work of the profession in general brings public good; therefore,
4. Adherence to the clause will bring more public good.

I want to suggest that few professionals would, or indeed should, be happy with the idea that the only ethical force in the principles in their codes comes indirectly through the possible promotion of cooperative endeavour, where having such cooperation is generally beneficial and in accordance with 'the presuppositions of ethics'. For instance, recklessly or maliciously injuring another member's reputation may well inhibit cooperation and lead to a loss of efficiency, but it is not bad only because it has those consequences, it would be a morally bad thing to do whether it had those consequences or not. To point out that in a particular case such injury had not, in fact, destroyed any cooperation or reduced efficiency would not be an adequate defence. Thus, I suggest that the kind of consequentialist view advocated by Davis fails to acknowledge just what it is about some of the clauses in codes of conduct that makes people want to describe them as 'ethical'.

Besides deontological and consequentialist moral theories, it is common to distinguish a third class: those based on a list of virtues. Again, some sort of case might be made out for saying that codes fit into a virtue based system. Many codes specifically mention virtues as ones to which members should conform. Examples include: integrity, honesty, fidelity, probity and impartiality. Of these only integrity is mentioned widely, and that often in a code's preamble. Integrity is not like virtues such as impartiality which can be applied only in limited circumstances, it applies to all other-regarding actions and even (in the view of philosophers like Sartre as well as Kant) to self-regarding ones. It belongs to that cluster of closely linked concepts which include 'acting in good faith', '. . . with a good will', or '. . . honourably', which lie at the heart of the Kantian ethics. Furthermore, most clauses in codes do not specifically mention virtues. Of course, not all virtues need have names, and one might coin names for each type of action advocated in a code. But it is this type of labour which is not required when fitting codes into a Kantian moral theory.

Why should codes be needed?

Having explained why, prima facie, it is plausible to give a Kantian interpretation to the principles in codes of conduct, I now want to discuss whether such a view can be sustained. In doing this I shall try to avoid raising contentious questions about how Kant's own views are to be interpreted. I shall argue that professional codes as they exist at present can be reconciled only with a corrupted version of Kant's theory, but that they could be improved by making them more compatible with his actual doctrines.

On a pure Kantian view why do we need codes at all? Surely a professional should make up his or her mind about how to act in good faith. There are two quite separate points here.

Firstly, Kant is not at all averse to setting down maxims in print. Notoriously, some of the examples he gives, such as the duty never to lie (Kant, 1979, p.363) are questionable candidates for what a rational will would adopt as universal laws of action. But my point here is that he does give examples and nothing he says would rule out our setting down a list of duties in a code as an aide-mémoire.

Most professions have drafted codes only in the last 30 years or so, but with a few exceptions the professions themselves have existed for much longer.

Although some codes have been introduced in direct response to cases of malpractice, many have been adopted because it is thought that with increasingly complex modes of work and with growing public scrutiny of professional behaviour, some set of guidelines will assist members to identify their duty. It is not that people generally acted unprofessionally before there were codes; what we get is a codification of existing good practice.

This brings me to the second point. Codes are drafted by committees consisting of a few members, but are to apply to a profession as a whole. They are not drawn up by an individual to help himself or herself. There is a problem here for the Kantian picture. It would seem to conflict with the personal autonomy central to his views, where responsibility is taken not only for one's actions but for deciding just what ones duty is. Thus the categorical imperative in the formula of universal law states: 'Act only on that maxim through which *you* can at the same time will that it should become a universal law' [my emphasis] (Kant, 1785, p. 84). We are to reason out maxims for ourselves not, as it were, take them off the shelf.

Kant would not be too worried about who first formulated a specific imperative of a code, for if it was a rational will, then any other rational will which thought things through should adopt a similar maxim. The risk is that people will not puzzle out maxims for themselves and so adopt them; rather, maxims will become externalized. Professionals may see a code as absolving them from the responsibility for determining their own duty. It could lead to actions not explicitly ruled out by the code being treated as permissible, even though they could not be sanctioned by the categorical imperative.

Some professional bodies do not have codes. This may be because they are in the fortunate position of not yet having had to worry about members acting unprofessionally. More often it is because they do not have powers of enforcement and so consider the adoption of one as a worthless exercise. Occasionally, however, the reason is more interesting. Until 1989 the Law Society of Scotland had no code and, until shortly before its demise, neither did the Press Council. Both for a long time preferred to deal with the majority of cases of unprofessional conduct on a basis like English common law, i.e. by building up a set of precedents, but also, occasionally, dealing with new types of case on first principles. As the Press Council remarked in one of its reports, it felt that at that time:

> . . . it was still preferable to rely on building up its jurisprudence rather than seek to reduce practice and ethics to a tight code. Partly it was conditioned in this view by the changes there are in public attitudes to conduct and to the press, and its view that it would be easier to reflect these in its adjudications without the constriction and formality of a more apparently permanent code. (Press Council, 1990, p. 286)

On Kantian grounds such a policy may be better than operating with a code. For it means that when there are no precedents, those adjudicating on possibly unethical conduct can decide the case by determining whether a rational will would consider that there was a duty to refrain from the action in question.

One of the troubles about having a code is that, however long, its set of clauses will not be comprehensive and, in particular, will not cover unprecedented sorts of unethical behaviour. Of course, new clauses can be added, but this takes time, and until it has been done the novel sort of unprofessional action will not be outlawed. It may even lead to a loophole-seeking mentality amongst some members of the profession. This is particularly likely to occur when behaving unethically can produce rich financial rewards.

A solution to this problem has been adopted by a small number of professional bodies. This is to state in the preamble to the code that its clauses cover only the more obvious types of unethical action from which members are to refrain, and that they are required to avoid committing unprofessional acts whether listed or not. Examples of bodies which have such preambles to their codes are The Royal Institution of Naval Architects, the Royal Pharmaceutical Society of Great Britain and the Royal Town Planning Institute. That of the Royal Pharmaceutical Society states:

110

Not all matters which should be subject to a standard of professional conduct are included in the Code; the matters mentioned are those upon which it is thought that guidance may be needed. The Council, in consideration whether or not action should be taken, do not regard themselves as being limited to those matters which are mentioned in this Code. (Harris, 1989, p. 277)

Nevertheless, even the introduction of this kind of open-ended rule may not prevent the dangers — from conventionalisation of the principles found in codes — that I refer to in the next section.

Restricted scope of application

Another questionable feature about trying to fit codes of conduct into a Kantian ethics is that the categorical imperative is supposed to be applied by every human agent. But a code is designed to be applied by members of a profession and by noone else. Of course, some Kantian precepts may be such that only a section of society can put them into practice. For instance, obligations to one's own children cannot be acted upon except by those who have become parents. But it is not that the codes for accountants or engineers apply to everyone, but are only acted upon by members of those professions; the codes have no force on anyone unless and until they become accountants or engineers.

The answer is, perhaps, that we should not see the contents of codes as Kantian moral principles, but rather as a set of guidelines about what maxims of action professional members should adopt, with the guidance being targeted only at them. Not maliciously harming the reputation of another is a plausible candidate for a moral imperative that everyone should follow, whether a professional or not. However, a professional body which puts a clause in its code about not harming another's reputation can address only its own members and may further limit its guidance to the time when members are acting in a professional capacity and the reputation being harmed is that of another member.

Some such guidelines appear unduly restrictive in their scope, especially in light of the danger of people taking as permissible what is not explicitly excluded. Why should it only be harm to the reputation of other *members* that is banned? Would it not be unethical to harm maliciously the reputation of, say, the *client* of another member? Some codes do have wider guidelines on this point and forbid harming the reputations of members *or others*. We can identify four categories of person who may be offered protection by a code: (1) members of a profession; (2) their clients; (3) individuals other than clients directly affected by a

111

professional's actions; (4) the general public. Codes which defend only the interests of (1) and (2) demonstrate a restrictiveness in concern which fits ill with Kantian, or indeed most other, moral theory.

One of the reasons professional ethics is seen as important is that the relationship between a member of a profession and a client is an unequal one. The professional is hired because he or she has expertise not possessed by the client. In the short term it may be impossible for the client to determine whether or not the expertise is being used competently or for his or her benefit. So those who seek professional help are forced to put their trust in those from whom they seek it. The interests of professionals will not be the same as those of their clients, but the latter should be able to trust the professionals not to act against their interests.

Clients who doubt whether professional codes do genuinely protect their interests could question the way most codes are drawn up. It is normal practice for codes to be drafted by committees consisting entirely of members of the profession concerned and so lacking representatives of clients or others who could be affected by professional action. Yet, who better to ensure that codes are worded so as to safeguard their interests than those whose interests they are?

A code should help to reconcile the interests of professionals and the clients and others whose actions they affect. This idea of acting in harmony with the interests of other people surfaces in Kant's conception of a 'kingdom' or 'commonwealth' of ends, which he describes as 'a whole of all ends in systematic conjunction', 'both of rational beings as ends in themselves and also of the personal ends which each may set before himself'. The guiding principle of this 'kingdom' is that a rational being 'should treat himself and all others, *never merely as a means*, but always *at the same time as an end in himself.*' (Kant, 1785, p. 95). A high proportion of the clauses from codes may be seen as applications of this rule, particularly regarding not treating clients as a means to advance personal ends of the professional.

The Kantian idea of treating another as an end in himself (or herself) carries the idea of doing the best one can for that other person within the constraints of universalisability. This, however, is not easy to reconcile with the way clauses in codes of conduct are, in practice, interpreted by at least some professionals. The trouble is that there can be clauses which are open to being interpreted as laying down *minimum* standards of conduct, rather than ones which will ensure the best possible treatment of the client.

Suppose, for instance, that a clause in a code requires a member who gives financial advice 'to declare any personal interest he or she has in any business referred to in the advice.'[2] The scope of the word 'personal' here is open to different possible interpretations. Narrowly, it might be taken to apply only to the member's own financial affairs and not to those of his or her wife or husband. If it is to be interpreted more widely, say, to include the interests of close relatives, how far is this to be taken? Often with such clauses conventions are established about how adjectives like 'personal', 'substantial', 'adequate', etc., are to be interpreted.

Imagine then that in my hypothetical case the convention is established that 'personal interest' encompasses the affairs of spouses and immediate blood relatives. This would then allow a member of the profession to refrain from disclosing a business interest of a live-in partner or of a step-daughter. Yet the existence of such an interest could, in a particular case, be just as relevant as those 'professionally required' to be disclosed. Here, rigid adherence to a conventionalized interpretation of the wording in a clause will produce a situation in which the interests of some clients will not be served in the best way possible, and hence doing so will mean treating the clause as other than a maxim expressing the categorical imperative. That is not to say that a member of the profession might not act as a good Kantian and declare an interest beyond the conventional scope, but my point is that the tendency to conventionalize interpretations of clauses encourages lower standards of conduct than those required by a pure Kantian ethics.

A final feature about most codes that demonstrates their limited application is that few have much to say about cases where someone in his or her leisure time acts in a way which, had he or she been at work, would have constituted unprofessional conduct. A noteworthy exception is the guide to conduct issued by the General Medical Council which states: 'The public reputation of the medical profession requires that every member should observe proper standards of personal behaviour, not only in his professional activities *but at all times*' [my italics]. (General Medical Council, 1987, p.13) The Scottish Faculty of Advocates also takes a principle that a lawyer should be worthy of the trust of those who deal with him or her to apply to 'an advocate's non-professional activities since his conduct there may affect the trust which others have in him in his professional capacity.' (Faculty of advocates, 1988, p.3) The relatively widely used requirement not to bring a profession 'into disrepute', even if taken to include non-professional activities, is likely to be seen as applicable only in respect of the most flagrant and well publicized misdeeds.

Conclusion

In the previous two sections I have argued that the clauses in existing professional codes, despite their imperatival form, are formulated and applied in ways which are hard to reconcile with Kantian moral theory. But given that it is even less plausible to base them on other types of moral theory, we might be led to the conclusion that they cannot be given any moral justification at all. This, I think, would be a mistake.

The defects or limitations in codes as they are now applied should not be taken to show that their clauses are not to be treated as Kantian principles at all, but rather that as Kantian principles they are flawed. So we should not look for a different theoretical basis, but try to ensure that codes fit the Kantian model better by seeking to rectify their current shortcomings.[3]

Notes

1. These were ones quoted verbatim in my *Professional codes of Conduct in the United Kingdom: A Directory* (1989). From my knowledge of professional codes used in other countries I have no reason to think that British codes are unique in displaying the features I discuss here.
2. I use a hypothetical example here, though one based on wording from actual codes, to avoid being accused of slandering members of some particular profession!
3. I should lke to express my thanks to participants at the May 1993 conference of the Society for Applied Philosophy, and also to John Kleinig, for helpful comments on an earlier version of this paper.

References

Davis, Michael (1991), 'Thinking like an engineer: the place of a code of ethics in the practice of a profession', Philosophy and public Affairs, vol 20.

Faculty of Advocates (1988), *Guide to the Professional Conduct of Advocates*, Faculty of Advocates, Edinburgh.

General medical Council (1987), *Professional Conduct and Discipline: Fitness to Practise*, General Medical Council, London.

Harris, N. (1989), *Professional Codes of Conduct in the United Kingdom: A Directory*, Mansell, London.

Kant, Immanuel (1797), *Uber ein vermeintes Recht aus Menschenliebe zu lügen*, translated by Thomas K. Abbot (1909) in *Kant's Critique of Practical Reason and Other Works*, 6th edition, Longmans, London.

Kant, Immanuel (1785), *Grundlegung zur Metaphysik der Sitten*, translated by H.J. Paton (1956) in *The Moral Law*, 3rd edition, Hutchinson, London.

Press Council (1990), *The Press and the People: 36th Annual Report (1989)*, The Press Council, London.

Production Engineer (1975), vl.54.

8 Common codes: Divergent practices

Jennifer Jackson

Codes of professional practice provide guidelines and requirements which are meant to be followed by all members of the profession. The purpose of such codes is indeed to establish and promulgate shared standards and 'agreed ways of handling cases' (MacIntyre, 1984, p. 511). But how far should we expect agreement in principle to be reflected in agreement in practice? And what counts as agreement in practice? Is it reasonable to expect all those professionals who sincerely subscribe and conform to a common code to act in the same way?

I shall argue that we should expect some uniformity but also some variation. I propose that we define 'same practice' to admit of variation in application but not of variation in interpretation. Whereas variation in how rules are applied is inevitable but innocuous, variation in how rules are interpreted subverts the purpose of codes and is neither unavoidable nor innocuous. If a common code is to be effective in sustaining shared values and principles within a profession, divergent practices among subscribers to the code cannot be tolerated. In order to eliminate these we (professionals and the informed public) need to engage in an ongoing dialogue in which we identify and study the problem areas. I shall indicate several such problem areas which characteristically underlie (and for a time may conceal) divergent practices.

Variations in application

It is inevitable that followers of the same rule will vary in how they apply it from case to case; the differing particularities of cases necessitate variation in how a rule is applied. Characteristically codes impose a number of obligations e.g. to respect your patients' dignity and to restore

116

them to health, and they impose obligations to distinct parties e.g. 'the prime concern of the clinical pharmacologist shall be welfare of both patient and public'. In some situations a choice of priorities has to be made e.g. putting patient before public or vice versa. You may have to attend to the particular case in all its specificity to judge which or whose interests should be preferred. Hence, as Aristotle long since observed, there is an ineliminable role for judgement (phronesis) in practical choice. Hence, the futility in seeking to replace juries' common sense judgements and judges' intuitions with an exhaustive criminal code — as Richard Tur has argued, 'the formulations to which legal science can aspire are necessarily defeasible in the face of ineffable circumstances.' (Tur, 1985, p. 82)

Moreover, even in regard to a particular case there are often alternative ways of following positive rules (you can pay your bill by cheque, in cash or with a postal order) and negative rules simply specify no-go areas leaving us otherwise free to roam elsewhere as suits. In other words, there is often no such thing as 'the right way' to follow a rule (e.g. the right way to make tea or make love) although some things are definitely wrong ways.

Suppose, for example, that you are a nurse and have been told to fetch a patient to be bathed or to have therapy; the patient refuses to comply — what ought you to do? There need not be 'the right thing for you to do' although obviously some things would be wrong — you ought not to slap or swear at the patient; you ought not to burst into tears or jump out the window. Probably if a student nurse anticipating this kind of question were to seek advice, the student would be told 'there are cases and cases' : sometimes one negotiates; sometimes one cajoles; sometimes one gives way. But even in regard to a particular case, there need not be such a thing as the right thing to say or do; one can imagine different nurses with different personalities adopting equally acceptable but different strategies.

Of course, we must not exaggerate the varieties of application. Sometimes there are no alternatives to select from if you are to follow the rule. If you are in the witness box, honesty may allow you no choice but to answer 'Yes' to a particular question. When Aristotle says that virtuous choice involves judgement we need not suppose that a conscious exercise of deliberation is always required — having judgement the possessor of virtue knows when deliberation is called for and when an appropriate choice needs no reflection.

Variation in application of rules in professional practice is not just something unavoidable that we have to put up with — it is something to be valued and safeguarded. Professionals need to be vigilant against calls for harmonization of their standards getting converted into attempts to curtail the role of professional judgement in decision making. There are, of course, situations in which there is such a thing as the correct procedure to follow — e.g. in using a fire extinguisher. But professional codes of practice range over more general constraints and aspirations. The constraints rule out certain ways of handling a situation. The aspirations allow scope for professional discretionary judgement, for variation in application case to case. Codes are not necessarily improved by being made more precise and specifically directive in what they prescribe.

Codes are often backed up with protocols. These though intended to encourage good practice can have the reverse effect on professionals. Some will trust the protocol when they should not; when they should not allow it to inhibit their professional discretionary judgement. Others will not trust the protocol when they should - having observed on particular occasions that the protocol is unduly restrictive, they cease to take its strictures seriously even when these do need to be adhered to.

To be sure the introduction of a variety of protocols dictating how tasks are to be done, protects the recipients of professional services from below standard service — or, at least, makes it easier for recipients of professional services to hold professionals to account — in principle, at any rate. Where we are generally confident that the professionals on whom we are relying are trustworthy we may be prepared to leave ourselves open to risk of bad (below standard) service if thereby we make it easier for the professionals to give as good (above standard) service. If, on the other hand, we are suspicious and cynical about the conduct of the professionals on whom we are relying we may be content to settle for managerial procedures which make both bad service and good service difficult — the former, intentionally, the latter, incidentally though forseeably.

Variations in interpretation

If we understand by the same practice, any practice which is an expression of the same principle or rule then, as we have noted, different actions can be instances of the same practice — of our agreement in practice. On the other hand, our doing the same action may convey a false impression, may mislead us into the wrong assumption that we are agreed in practice, that we are following the same rule, when in fact we are not. Our concurrence in the same action might be quite coincidental.

Agreement in practice requires that we interpret the rule with which we are complying in the same way. Suppose, for example, that we all say we subscribe to a principle of equality, to the idea that all interests deserve equal consideration. Upon probing, it might turn out that our agreement is quite spurious — as if, e.g. we differ in our interpretation of what kind of entity can have interests: some of us might say, 'only people' (or,

118

darkly, 'only people who are "persons"'); others might say, 'any sentients' while still others might also ascribe interests to certain non- sentients e.g. to plants, to rivers. And what about future generations — does the principle apply to the interests of people who do not yet exist? These variations in interpretation are not alternative ways of applying the same rule. Rather, they would show that there was not one rule which we all endorsed.

Since different actions do not necessarily betoken divergent practices, the fact that we do differ with our professional colleagues may go undetected for a time. If we then discover that our trust in one another has been misplaced, that we do not after all share the same understanding of the code we endorse i.e. that we do not actually have a common code, we may unreasonably suspect one another of hypocrisy. Hence the importance of maintaining an ongoing dialogue in which we seek to clarify our interpretation of the code and to achieve a genuine consensus on what it should be.

It may be unrealistic to expect everyone to be in complete agreement as to what the code of a particular profession should be. In a way, though, open disagreement is less damaging to a profession than hidden unacknowledged variations in interpretation. Where we cannot, (for the time being anyway) agree, we can compromise in a fudge — as codes often do. We are not then surprised to find within the profession divergent practices in relation to the fudged items — e.g., to 'the first moral principle imposed upon the physicians is respect for human life from its beginning' (Declaration of Oslo, 1983). It is common knowledge that there is sharp dissension among doctors, nurses and the public at large as to when human life should be deemed to begin.

Divergent practices

One aspect of codes which generates confusion, which obscures variations in interpretation, is our failure to distinguish goal related aspirational obligations from obligations imposing side-constraints on how goals are to be pursued. Some items in a code are clearly aspirational and open-ended obligations viz. those which express the aims of the profession e.g. to restore health, to relieve suffering. If you are a nurse or a doctor you are entitled to make choices in pursuance of these goals over how, where and when you comply: e.g. whether you relieve the suffering of young patients or old, whether you do so at home or at school, full time or part time.

Other items in a code specify certain side-constraints on how the goals of the profession are to be pursued. In seeking to restore health or prevent illness, e.g., nurses are obliged to respect their patients' dignity and to keep confidences. These constraints are boundary fixing, they specify the ground rules which are supposed to govern all the nurse's professional dealings. Thus a nurse is not supposed to pick and choose whose confidences to keep or which patients to treat with dignity.

Yet it is not always clear whether a particular item in a code falls in the one category or the other. Consider the obligation just mentioned 'to treat patients with dignity'. Some nurses might regard that obligation as aspirational — one of the aims to be pursued alongside the others whereas others would regard this obligation not as itself an aim but rather as a constraint on the pursuit of their professional aims. We might expect that those who adopted the former view would be readier to impose on their patients, to intervene paternalistically, than the latter.

Compare the effect, for example, of regarding the obligation on doctors to get informed consent to invasive treatment or research — is this an aspirational obligation — one of the things that you try to do? Should it jostle alongside your other obligations e.g. to advance medical knowledge, to benefit this patient etc., or, is it a constraint on these other aims? Two doctors might sincerely agree that they have a duty to get informed consent but have divergent practices reflecting just this kind of difference in how they interpret the obligation; in the kind of obligation they take it to be.

Variations in interpretation may also be explained by different understanding of the sources of our obligations. We may all agree that doctors should be honest with their patients and yet we might have quite different ideas about why they ought to be honest. For a time, the differences might not surface. And it might be supposed that the sources of an obligation need not be explored by the busy professional — leave that to the philosophers! But sooner or later divergent practices may be expected to surface since what an obligation requires, what it involves, depends in part on why it matters.

Does being honest with patients mean never lying to them or does it mean only lying to them when it is 'necessary' (therapeutic privilege)? Does the duty to be 'open' with patients mean answering all their questions truthfully and fully? Does it mean, in addition, correcting their misperceptions e.g. their unrealistic hopes, whether caused by ourselves or our colleagues or their relatives?

There are a number of reasons why doctors may be said to have a duty to be honest. It is often said that honesty is required just because it is best policy i.e. the most effective management strategy in relation to the aims of restoring health/relieving suffering. Honesty with dying patients will not effect a cure but it may be said to ease their dying, to enable them to come to terms with their predicament and to make the most of what life remains.

Now if this is the only source of the obligation on doctors to be honest with patients, the obligation is not a constraint on the general aims of medicine: there is no conflict between being honest and benefiting the patient. But notice that so interpreted the obligation to be honest is conditional: it applies only where truthfulness is the more effective strategy — as it may be with the dying but not necessarily with all patients in all circumstances e.g. not, perhaps, with anorexics.

Suppose, alternatively, the source of the obligation to be honest is thought to be the patients' right to decide for themselves what treatments they undergo, what drugs they imbibe etc. Then, doctors who withheld information from patients to prevent them making choices detrimental to their own health would be violating their rights.

Here again, what doctors take to be the source of their obligation to be honest (and open) can make a difference to what they take the obligation to require. If the duty derives from a right, then the right may be waived (some patients ask their doctors to choose for them); and some patients may be too ill to exercise the right.

There are other possible sources of the obligation to be honest. Self-determination may be said to be not a right but a duty — in which case patients should not be allowed to waive it, to fob off the burden of choice onto their doctors' shoulders. Or again, the obligation might be said to arise from the fiduciary relationship between doctor and patient — how can trust be preserved if doctors are not committed to truthfulness?

Leaving aside consideration of the particular merits of these alternative accounts, the point I wish to make is that whichever account we favour has practical implications. Hence, the discussion of sources, how the obligation (if it exists) should be grounded, is not only of interest for philosophers and for doctors/nurses who happen to have a philosophical bent. Since the source of the obligation affects what complying with it involves, professionals who attribute the obligation to different sources can be expected to diverge in practice.

In the recent revised handbook on medical ethics published by the BMA, *Philosophy and Practice* (BMA, 1988) the authors begin by distancing the professional's interest in ethics from the philosopher's. The authors observe that doctors come into the profession from different backgrounds and can be expected to have different reasons, some religious, some philosophical, for subscribing to items in the common code. The merits of these various religious and philosophical groundings, we are told, need not be explored: they are irrelevant to practice. In this, I suggest, the authors are mistaken. Readers of such handbooks may gain a false sense of security — 'This is our code to which we are all bound' — only to find in due course and to their dismay that fellow subscribers interpret items of the code differently and engage in divergent practices.

The truth is: an unexamined code is not worth having.

Might it, though, be possible to improve a code to the point that there would be no further need for ancillary dialogue over its interpretation? It would not. While some ambiguities and vagueness might be removed — as a consequence of constructive dialogue, a professional code cannot be refined so as to make its interpretation throughout self-evident. There will always have to be included phrases the meaning of which must be studied in relation to actual practice and to the understandings of practitioners familiar with the traditions of their profession — phrases like 'so far as is reasonably practicable' (e.g., in regard to the Health and Safety Act at Work, 1974) and 'the highest standards of nursing care possible within the reality of a specific situation' (from the UKCC Code of Professional Conduct, 1992). We need to attach such qualifiers to many of the side-constraint requirements in a code just because it is predictable that exceptional circumstances will occur although what these will be cannot be spelled out precisely in advance.

Generating constructive dialogue

Variations in interpretations of codes need to be corrected and so far as possible prevented — sooner or later, if there are differences, they will surface and make for trouble. How, though, can differences be avoided or overcome? I have said that there needs to be ongoing dialogue not just with a view to regular revisions of a code's wording, but to sustain a genuinely shared understanding of a code's meaning.

How can such a dialogue be achieved? Is it feasible for professionals to engage in such a dialogue across national, religious and cultural boundaries? The meaning, the interpretation, of a rule has to be learned in part through participation in a common tradition. This participation has to be of experienced professional practitioners since it is only through practice that the rules whose interpretation is problematic can be understood. Thus novices to a profession, no matter how eagerly and conscientiously they have studied its code in advance, learn the code's interpretation only on the job. Its interpretation is something that has to be observed and absorbed through practice: 'Not only rules, but also examples are needed for establishing a practice. Our rules have loop-holes open, and the practice has to speak for itself' (Wittgenstein, 1969, p.139).

This necessity that the practice must speak for itself is, as we have noted, neither avoidable nor regrettable. But it does give us reason to question the possibility of achieving a common tradition of professionals, a tradition that is espoused and followed by the membership worldwide. Practice, after all, always takes place in a specific environment: a particular clinic, a hospice, an institution. Is it possible for professionals to extrapolate from their own individual practising contexts to maintain genuine dialogue in developing common standards? If you are a wise and good member of your profession in one part of the world should you be able to practise just as effectively elsewhere provided only you are proficient in languages or have an interpreter at your elbow?

People are able to take part in sport, to play games, following the same rules with a shared understanding of how they are to be interpreted although the participants come from a multiplicity of cultures and countries. Is it equally feasible for professionals to share an understanding of the rules which govern their professional lives?

One important respect in which engaging in sporting activity abroad is disanalogous to engaging in professional activity abroad is that the former activity is characteristically public and visible whereas the latter is characteristically private and hidden. Confidentiality is a prominent duty in professional activity: clients' privacy has to be protected. Thus while we can all observe how foreign sportsmen play golf or football, it is much more difficult for us to observe how, for example, foreign doctors, prison officers or engineers operate on a day to day basis — how they interpret the rules governing the way they are enacting their professional duties. Moreover, although the connection between certain sporting activities and people's sense of cultural or national identity can run deep, the rules of play are often unproblematic — these are readily accessible to people from a variety of different backgrounds. The interpretation of rules governing professional activities tends to be more problematic, more embedded in cultural attitudes and religious beliefs. Consider, for instance, how one's attitude to death must be affected by one's religious beliefs or lack of them. It might make all the difference to one's future prospects, if one were dying, whether one died one way rather than another. Who of us if we believed that a blood transfusion would debar us from eternal bliss would settle for a transfusion merely to eke out a while longer our earthly existence?

It stands to reason then that the more culturally and religiously diverse members of a profession are, the more difficult it must be for them to share standards — and the more risk there is that they may be innocently tricked into rashly assuming that because all members put their names to the same code document with honest intent, there exists among them a shared understanding of standards.

A final point. For whom is a code of practice written? Is it written for those outside the profession as a political weapon — staking out what the profession deems to be minimal standards in keeping with the profession's aims, so that members can proceed to clamour for the resources they need to enable them to comply with their code? Or, is the code written rather for those inside the profession, setting forth the guidelines and requirements that they can be expected to follow in their day to day practice? No doubt the codifiers would wish their code to serve both needs. But there is a difficulty in seeking to influence both audiences through the same document.

Professionals' respect for their code may be subverted when they notice that it includes as requirements specific obligations which they know perfectly well they regularly cannot conform to under existing circumstances. How can a code be taken seriously if it includes some requirements which as things stand are ridiculous — e.g. requiring that all patients are to be given full counselling 'appropriate to their needs'? The actual logistics, the number of patients, turn over of patients and number of qualified clinicians may make nonsense of this as a requirement.

There is a danger then that once a written code is discredited, practising professionals will take instead for their guidelines the standards which happen to prevail wherever they work — and these may well sink below the standards it is reasonable to expect professionals to conform to even under existing circumstances.

References

British Medical Association (1988), *Philosophy and Practice of Medical Ethics*, British Medical Association, London.

MacIntyre, Alasdair (1984), 'Does applied ethics rest on a mistake?' *Monist*, vol. 67.

Tur, Richard (1985), 'Dishonesty and the jury: a case study in the moral content of law' in Phillips Griffiths, A. (ed.), *Philosophy and Practice*, Cambridge University Press, Cambridge.

Wittgenstein, Ludwig (1969) *On Certainty*, edited by Anscombe, G.E.M. and von Wright, G.H., Blackwell, Oxford.

9 Narrating social work

Andrew Edgar

Codes of ethics and of conduct exist to provide a guide for the professional as to the limits of acceptable ethical behaviour, and if necessary to ground disciplinary action against the professional.[1] The interpretation of a code must therefore involve a recognition of the applicability of any particular tenet of the code to the concrete circumstances of everyday professional activity. Yet the 'correct' interpretation of a code will rarely, if ever, be self-evident. As the code of the British Association of Social Workers notes, '[t]he Code of Ethics cannot be a manual of practice guidance. It must be couched in general terms, without being so general as to be incapable of application' (BASW, 1985, p. 4 (Commentary on the Code of Ethics, paragraph 3)). Having posed this problem the BASW code continues to provide a partial solution by distinguishing between its 'statement of principles' and 'principles of practice', the latter being 'more personal and in more concrete terms. They move from general principles to guide practice' (BASW, 1985, p. 6 (On its principles of practice)). This is unsatisfactory. A gap remains between the principles and the concrete situation. It may be suggested that the structures of the codes of the National Association of Social Workers and BASW manifest different approaches to this problem. The NASW's concern with the interpretation of the code focuses on its application, and so provides a separate gloss on each of its major principles, thereby increasing their specificity. In contrast, BASW is seemingly concerned with the interpretative understanding of the code as a whole. Its paragraphs of commentary do not treat the code's principles as necessarily separate items. The commentary serves to establish themes that recur and so interweave the elements of the code, thereby grounding the reader's approach to the code as a whole. Yet neither of these approaches ultimately bridges the gap between code and reality. For

125

BASW 'personal judgement' (BASW, 1985, p. 6), and for NASW an individual's anticipation of 'the judgement of an unbiased jury of professional peers' (Code of Ethics of the National Association, 1987, p. 951 (Preamble)) both of which appear to be beyond codification, are necessary to complete this bridge.

A frequent criticism put against codes is that they lack a coherent grounding in ethical theory. This may be seen as being in part a response to the fundamental indexicality[2] of codes. If a code were to be clearly and consistently derived from, for example, consequentialism or a rights theory, then the interpretation of the code might be clarified. I wish to suggest that this would represent a misunderstanding of how codes are, and indeed should be written, interpreted and applied. The BASW code appeals to rights (although principally the legal rights of a citizen), duties and obligations, needs and welfare, with little apparent recognition of the weight that is given to these terms in ethical theory. Even the appeal to principles is misleading. The deductive rigour of say, Beauchamp and Childress's (1979) principlism, is missing. It may be suggested that the codes' principles are little more than expressions of underlying value orientations. The most basic ethical principle offered by the BASW is 'the recognition of the value and dignity of every human being' (BASW, 1985, p. 2 (Statement of principles, paragraph 6)). The NASW code similarly includes 'the worth, dignity, and uniqueness of all persons' amongst the 'fundamental values' of the profession (Code of the National Association, p. 951 (Preamble)). In partial clarification of what is meant by 'value', the 1976 report on social work education, *Values in Social Work*, notes that 'notions of health, normality, maturity ... and even "basic needs" are frequently taken for granted without considering the value positions they reflect. To call someone sick or mentally ill ... immature ... or deprived often acquires the authority of a factual statement because the abstract values upon which such descriptions are grounded are so frequently assumed' (CCETSW, 1976, p. 12). In sum, it is presupposed that the social worker has values which orientate his or her judgement and description of the facts of a case, and thus of the client to whom those facts are relevant, and that such value orientations must be explicated.

The problem of a code's indexicality is, therefore, not overcome through the further specification of general principles, but rather by recognising that professionals already understand their practice in terms of moral values. (In effect, the problem is not one of analysing objectively described moral dilemmas through the application of general principles, akin to the scientific explanation of a fact through application of a universal law, but one of hermeneutic interpretation, involving a circle between the already interpreted particular and the general horizon of interpretation brought to it (Ricoeur, 1981, pp. 275-7). Codes serve to challenge or confirm the moral understanding that the professional already has, not by immediately subjecting that understanding to a test of logical coherence according to a given ethical theory, but by requiring the explication of that understanding. It may be suggested that this explication occurs in the predominantly narrative accounts that professionals can give of their actions. Codes provide frameworks which guide and structure, not the professionals' practice as such, but rather the retrospective or prospective accounts that professionals can legitimately give of their practice. The codes frame specifically ethical narratives of mundane practice. If the professional's behaviour can be narrated within the terms proposed by the code, then the behaviour is legitimated; if not, it is censured. The consideration of codes as narrative frameworks has a number of specific consequences, not merely for the account of the bridge that they establish to reality, but also for their assessment as ethical documents. It is being suggested that codes place specific restrictions upon the way in which a professional can provide a moral account of his or her behaviour. These restrictions may be seen to focus upon a number of distinctive aspects of narrative.[3]

A narrative will typically have characters (who may be individual human beings, or such social institutions as organizations, classes and nations, or even nonhuman creatures). Characters will have specific capacities, goals and abilities, moral strengths and weaknesses. A narrative will have a narrator (who, as the 'point of view' from which the story is told, is distinct from the empirical author). In that the narrator does not and cannot aspire to a position of neutrality or objectivity in relation to the events narrated, the point of view adopted entails a specific judgement of the events (Ricoeur, 1981, p. 279). This judgement is articulated in what Ricoeur terms the 'configuration' of a series of events, actions and interactions, actors and motives, circumstances and outcomes within a plot. Configuration requires more than the mere chronological recounting of otherwise isolated events. Rather, it serves to bring the diverse events into a meaningful whole. The whole is the point, theme or idea of the account. Each event thereby acquires sense only through being placed and grasped in specific relationships to other events within the narrative (Ricoeur, 1984, p. 65). This emplotment is centrally seen in terms of a relationship between discordance and concordance, such that the narrative contains within itself disruptive events, threatening the whole with disorder and meaninglessness (Ricoeur, 1984, pp. 72-3). In a predominantly moral narrative, the discordance of the story will be the articulation of the moral problem itself. This contingency (such that, unfolding over time, the events could have been otherwise) is overcome insofar as the conclusion of the story is 'acceptable after all' (Ricoeur, 1981, p. 277). (While an acceptable conclusion will make sense of the events narrated, it is never the only possible, nor even necessarily the most satisfactory conclusion. In this it is distinct from a predictable conclusion, deduced through the application of general principles.)

It is here being suggested that codes of ethics allow for particular types of character (by embodying a particular description of the profession, the individual professional, the client and possibly other professionals with whom the social worker must cooperate), a particular point of view from which the moral narrative is told, and a particular configuration of the narrative's plot. In order to account for their actions, the mundane and superficially heterogeneous events of social workers' practices must be synthesized, or configured, into a meaningful whole. The emplotment demanded by a code of ethics, precisely insofar as it specifies the sort of discordance that will count as the material of an ethical narrative, serves to articulate the concept of ethics that can be legitimately held within the profession.

The characters proposed by the BASW and NASW codes are in some contrast. While both separate the professional from the private citizen (BASW, 1985, p. 1 (Foreword, paragraph 2); Code of Ethics of the National Association, 1987, p. 953 (Principles I.a.1 & 3)), NASW places heavy emphasis upon this. The practitioner is divided against him or herself, with professional integrity being pitched against personal interests and desires. In effect the code lists the temptations to which the professional may fall prey. Warning that certain forms of private conduct may compromise 'the fulfilment of professional responsibilities' (NASW, 1987, p. 953 (Principles I.A.1.)) and of the possible inhibition of the exercise of professional discretion and impartiality (p.953 (Principles I.D.1)) the code proceeds to detail examples of such conduct and inhibition, including fraud and deceit (p. 953 (Principles I.A.2 and I.D.2)); the misrepresentation of professional qualifications and competencies (pp. 953, 956 (Principles I.B.1 and V.M.4)); sexual involvement with clients (p. 954 (Principles II.F.5); exploitation of disputes between colleagues (p.955 (Principles III.J.6)); and the misuse of the employer's resources (p. 955 (Principles IV.L.4)). (The negative tone of this portrait is balanced at specific points. The professional is someone who 'should work to improve ... [an] agency's policies and procedures', recognize NASW sanctions, and work to prevent discrimination (p. 955 (Principles IV.L.1-2)). This includes a responsiblity to advocate government policy changes and encourage public debate on policy (P. 956 (Principles VI.P.6-7)). In sum, he or she should protect and enhance the dignity and integrity of the profession and should be responsible and vigorous in discussion and criticism of the profession ((p. 956 (Principles V.M.1)).

The NASW professional is thereby portrayed within a familiar liberal model of human being. The sensuous, or private, self is pitted against the rational, or public, self. A key but largely undefined, concept in the code is that of 'integrity'. Negatively, the individual professional's integrity is threatened by his or her private self, and yet positively the individual strives to maintain the integrity of the profession as a whole. Integrity may be understood in terms of autonomy. Professionalism aspires to an objectivity in opposition to the individual's subjectivity. Professionalism is not thereby seen to be value neutral, but is rather focussed by the defining values of the profession 'that include the worth, dignity, and uniqueness of all persons' (p. 951 (Preamble)). A position of integrity is one uninfluenced by heterogeneous forces and values, and is thus 'impartial' (p. 952 (Summary I.D.)). The professional, represented by 'an unbiased jury of professional peers', is the guardian of this autonomy, so that the individual maintains his or her professional (or rational) status by submitting to, and engaging with, the authority of the profession.

The BASW code offers a more subtle and ironic series of portraits. The tension between the private and the professional is noted, but not made thematic. Indeed, it is accepted that the professional will be able to judge when private interests — 'for example, as a citizen or parent' (BASW, 1985, p. 7 (On principle 6)) — legitimately take precedence. A complex image is described in the four part statement of principles. This covers professionals' moral beliefs (centring upon recognition of the value and dignity of all), objectives (of enhancing human wellbeing), commitment and skill, and most importantly their position within social and political structures. This position is boldly presented as 'the interface between powerful organisations and relatively powerless applicants for service' (BASW, 1985, p. 2). To be embedded in these, and other more insidious, power structures, leaves the social worker acutely, and self-consciously, vulnerable to failure. This point recurs throughout the code. The social worker's individual limitations embrace professional competence, either in terms of the inadequacy of training and experience, or of the profession's knowledge base (BASW, 1985, pp. 2,6,7 (Statement of principles 8; On its principles of practice; On principles 7 & 8)) and the inevitability of prejudice (BASW,1985, p.7 (On principle 3)). Social and political limitations compound this problem, ultimately serving to qualify the objectives of the profession, for the worker must recognize the practical limitations that impede achievement (BASW, 1985, p. 7 (On principle 7)) and the restrictions that 'real-life situations' place upon the client's self-realisation (BASW, 1985, p. 7 (On principle 6)). Even the encouragement to engage in politics is qualified, for 'the opportunity to contribute to the formulation of policies may ... be extremely limited' (BASW, 1985, p. 6 (On its principles of practice)). Finally the 'interface' at which the professional stands is 'where contacts take place, contacts ... which may lead to harmony or tó conflict' ((BASW, 1985, p. 7 (On paragraph 9)). The reality and possible irresolvability of conflict is stressed in the client's relationship to others, as well as in the professional's relationship to the client (BASW, 1985, p. 7 (On principle 5)). In sum, while the NASW code presents an essentially autonomous agent, striving to overcome the impediments of heterogeneity, the BASW presents the agent as being inevitably embedded in social and political structures. While 'integrity' is synonymous with autonomy in the NASW code, for the BASW 'integrity' is working to the best of one's ability (BASW, 1985, pp. 2&3 (Principle 8, and Principles of practice)).

This difference is compounded by the BASW portrait of the client. Necessarily, the position of the client is complementary to that of the professional. The professional's goals are defined by, or ascribed to, the client. The NASW code says little of the client. Nothing serves to differentiate the position of the client from that of any other citizen. They have interests, legally defined rights, and may suffer harm. They are ultimately capable of 'self-determination' (Code of Ethics of the National Association, 1987, p. 954).The BASW code rejects the use of 'self-determination'; because the term 'sounds a little too open-ended', and fails 'to recognise the limitations which real-life situations impose' (BASW, 1985, p. 5 (On paragraph 6)). Similarly, the social worker's responsibilities are weighed with respect to the 'client's frequent lack of power' (BASW, 1985, p. 6 (On paragraph 9)). Ultimately, the client is separated from the ordinary citizen. It is acknowledged that the social work client is a construction, the product of social processes, such that the individual concerned may suffer a 'loss of dignity or rights by the very act of becoming a client' (BASW, 1985, p. 6 (On principle 2).

It is from these characters, of professional, client, and more illusively the profession itself, that the emplotment of the respective ethical narratives of NASW and BASW may be derived. In effect, the above accounts reveal two distinctive conceptions of what ethics is, and thus of the relevance of ethics to the profession, the way which ethical problems can be articulated and resolved, and the manner in which the gap between reality and code is bridged.

NASW focuses ethical issues on the threat that the private individual poses to the profession. The problems of the structural determination and construction of the client's predicament are marginalized. The professional's responsibilities to society are summarized in seemingly unproblematic terms, such that the 'social worker should act to prevent and eliminate discrimination', ensure access to resources, expand client choice, promote diversity of cultures, provide emergency services, advocate policy change and encourage public participation in policy formation (Code of Ethics of the National Association, 1987, p. 956 (Principles VI.P.1-7). While this section of the code stretches ethics beyond the merely personal, it continues to presuppose an autonomous individual acting upon society, not an individual acted upon and constructed by society. It thereby excludes the possibility of a meaningful ethical narrative exploring the professional's, or the client's, continued failure and lack of integrity. This does not necessarily entail that NASW excludes such narratives altogether; merely, that it cannot understand them as ethical narratives. This is coherent with the earlier assertion that moral dilemmas are always already described in value laden terms. To describe an event as a moral problem already presupposes a certain approach to ethics.

The BASW code, in marked contrast to NASW's, centres ethics on the instability of mundane practice, and grounds this instability, conflict and failure in social factors. The focus of ethics becomes the involuntary vulnerability of the client, not the possible wilful immorality of the professional. This broadens the scope of ethical narratives, not merely by allowing the inclusion of more events and a wider range of approaches to those events, but also by allowing for superficially unsatisfactory conclusions. Failure may be 'acceptable after all' as the outcome of an ethical narrative.

Michael W. Whan has appealed to Northrop Frye's fourfold classification of genres in order to analyse the function of narrative in social work. These four are the tragic, romantic, comic and ironic. 'In tragedy, time appears as inexorable ... creating a feeling of nemesis. In the romantic tale, it is full of nostalgia... The comic sense of time is one of progress, improvements in spite of or even because of difficulty and crisis, timely providence, overcoming, redeeming growth, ultimate trust and optimism. With irony there is an awareness of the all-too-human, an appreciation of paradox, surprise and limitation, a readiness for sudden fateful change, and an acceptance of predicament and even failure' (Whan, 1979, pp. 489-99, 492-3). It may be concluded that the NASW code is comic, while the BASW code is ironic.

Consideration of the position of the narrator opens a final level of analysis, not least by indicating the implicit internal politics of the social work profession. If codes provide a narrative framework, then they may determine the point of view from which the story is told. This is distinct from asking after the identity of the author of a particular code, albeit that it is a related question. The analysis may be developed by recognizing the relationship between the individual professional and the professional association, and so in effect between the author of a narrative and the author of a code.

The BASW code is prefaced by the following note: 'The Code which follows was adopted by BASW at the Annual General Meeting, Edinburgh, 1975. All members of the Association are required to uphold the Code'. Implicit in this is the tension between a profession's governing association and the governed members. On the one hand it is asserted that the code has been adopted, presumably voluntarily, by the Association; on the other it is asserted that the code is to be imposed upon all members of the Association. The status of the Association thereby shifts uneasily between the collective voice of the profession, and a governing body that stands aloof from its membership. This interpretation is compounded by the fifth paragraph of the code: 'Any professional association has the duty to secure, as far as possible that its members discharge their professional obligations; and that members are afforded in full necessary professional rights' (BASW, 1985, p. 1). The ambiguity of the status of the Association is of central reference to the question of the narrator facilitated by the code. If the code is an expression of the collective voice of the profession, then any narrative presented within the framework of the code is the autobiography of the professional. If the Association governs its members, and the code is imposed and enforced by the Association, any narrative posed within the code's framework is underwritten by this power relationship. Individual members, using the code to justify their actions, do so within an imposed framework. Their attempts to provide their own narrative of their own actions are undermined by the intrusion of another voice. Their autobiographies are actually biographies.

If the code was presented as an overtly disciplinary tool (and thus as a code of conduct) this would be less problematic. As a document in ethics, particularly insofar as that document recognizes the instability of mundane professional practice, the code is concerned with the need to facilitate change within the profession. The code refers to the need for 'the constant evaluation of methods and policies' in the light of social and professional change (BASW, 1985, p. 2 (Principle 8)). and in consequence the provisional status of any code (BASW, 1985, p. 4 (Commentary on paragraph 1)). The NASW code makes a bolder statement, requiring the social worker to 'be responsible and vigorous in discussion and criticism of the profession' (Code of Ethics of the National Association, p. 956 (Principles V.M.1). The NASW code thereby poses the basic problem of who determines the limits of responsible criticism?

This question can be reworked. If the fundamental problem of codes of ethics (and of conduct) is that of correct interpretation, and thus of the bridging of the gap between code and reality, one may ask who decides that a given interpretation is correct? By requesting responsible criticism, NASW opens up the possibility of members providing new and diverse interpretations, and yet subordinates that freedom to the authority of the professional association. The NASW code further inscribes this tension in its 'Preamble'. Practitioners are required to take into account, not merely the particular principles, 'but also the entire code and its spirit'. The appeal to spirit marks the limits of what can be codified. The arbiter of this spirit is the 'unbiased jury of professional peers'. While this phrase refers to a consensus position within the profession, and thus to the possibility of professional change and development, the emphasis on the lack of bias, and by association the central, and under-articulated concept of 'integrity', serves to fix the core values of the profession as being beyond ethical debate. The narrator must be unbiased, and so demonstrate integrity, for his or her narrative to be acceptable.

BASW acknowledges a similar opposition between the letter and the spirit of a code. 'Personal responsibility' is assumed to be 'crucial to professionalism. A completely bureaucratised service cannot be a professional one, (BASW, 1985, p. 7 (On principle 7)). Unlike the NASW code, however, the relationship between the individual professional and the profession (or professional association) goes unarticulated. The presumption that the code speaks with the collective voice of the profession, or that the narrator is unproblematically a 'Member of the Association' (BASW, 1985, p. 3 (Principles of practice)) again undermines the possibility of a critical distance from its expression of fundamental values, so inhibiting the possibility of a legitimate narrative of fundamental change.

In conclusion, it may be suggested that the very project of a code of ethics is problematic. The BASW and NASW codes implicitly acknowledge that the problem of the interpretation of the code cannot be overcome by the codes themselves. Interpretation rests upon that which cannot be codified. The codes thereby serve to put the grounds of interpretation outside of the scope of their own (ethical) criticism. This may briefly be analysed by appeal to the concept of a narrative tradition (Ricoeur, 1984; pp. 68-70, 76-7; 1986, pp. 207-40; 1981, pp. 286-7). A tradition serves to ground, through historical transmission, that which is acceptable and therefore meaningful in a given narrative form. Traditions accrue from the sedimentation of the configurational grammar of a narrative (such that certain ways of narrating a story, including ways of articulating characters and plot, are passed, as givens, from one generation to the next). But traditions also facilitate innovation. On the one hand, a tradition cannot determine the detail of the singular work which is produced within it. On the other hand, the rules and forms embodied in the tradition provide the basis for meaningful innovation and change. It is precisely this change that maintains the vitality of the tradition. A profession will be underpinned by its own traditions[4] and it is precisely the ethical tradition to which a code should appeal in order to ground its interpretation and reinterpretation. The NASW and BASW codes corrupt this relationship by diverting their grounding to the professional associations. The failure to make the relationship of code and tradition explicit serves to cut short the interplay between sedimentation and innovation. A code of ethics thereby becomes parasitic upon the tradition (rather than being the focus for its renewal). While drawing upon the tradition (as that which is beyond the code) for their interpretation and application, the NASW and BASW codes implicitly proscribe the innovatory potential of their traditions, by preventing a new interpretation of the profession's ethics from feeding back into the tradition. Innovation is thereby marginalized or rejected. Unless a code can be so formulated as to allow genuine criticism, it remains the pure sedimentation of a tradition, and as such contributes to the reproduction of the existing politics of the profession.

Notes

1. See 'Preamble' to the 'Code of Ethics of the National Association of Social Workers' in Minahan, Anne et al., (eds), (1987) *The Encyclopaedia of Social Work*, 18th edition, National Association of Social Workers, Silver Spring, Maryland, Appendix 1, p. 951.
2. In the definition offered by D. Lawrence Wieder, an indexical expression is such that its 'meaning is relative to such contextual matters as (a) who was saying it...; (b) to whom it was being said...; (c) where it was being said...; (d) on what occasion it was being said...; (e) the social relationship between teller and hearer...; and so forth'. See Lawrence Wieder, 'Telling the Code' in Turner, Roy (ed.), (1974), *Ethnomethodology*, Penguin, Harmondsworth, pp. 161-2.
3. The approach to narrative adopted here is drawn from Paul Ricoeur. See his 'The Narrative Function' and *Time and Narrative*, translated by Kathleen McLaughlin and David Pellauer (1984, 1985 and 1986), Chicago University Press, Chicago and London.
4. See Edgar, Andrew (1993), 'Nursing as a Moral Tradition', *Journal of Advances in Health and Nursing Care*, vol. 2, no. 3, pp. 3-20, for a development of this approach through appeal to the work of Alasdair MacIntyre.

References

Beauchamp, T.L. and Childress, J.F. (1979), *Principles of Biomedical Ethics*, Oxford University Press, New York.
British Association of Social Workers (BASW) (1985), 'A Code of Ethics

for Social Work' in Watson, David (ed.), *A Code of Ethics for Social Work: The Second Step*, Routledge & Kegan Paul, London.

Central Council for Education and Training in Social Work (CCETSW) (1976), *Values in Social Work*, CCETSW, London.

Code of Ethics of the National Association (1987), in Minahan, Anne et al., (eds), *The Encyclopaedia of Social Work*, 18th edition, National Association of Social Workers, Silver Spring, Maryland.

Ricoeur, Paul (1981), 'The Narrative Function' in his *Hermeneutics and the Human Sciences*, edited and translated by J.B. Thompson, Cambridge University Press, Cambridge.

Ricoeur, Paul (1984, 1985, 1986), *Time and Narrative*, translated by Kathleen McLaughlin and David Pellauer, Chicago University Press, Chicago and London.

Whan, Michael W. (1979), 'Accounts, Narrative and Case History', *British Journal of Social Work*, vol. 9, no.4.

10 The nature and role of professional codes in modern society

Heta and Matti Häyry

The existence of professions and professionals is based on human needs, desires, preferences, values and interests. The needs and values of human beings, combined with our beliefs and material surroundings, form the foundation of all social life, and social life can in some degree be defined by the division of labour among individuals and groups. The advanced division of labour, in its turn, has in many cases led to the emergence of professions and professionals. The connection between needs and professional life is presented in a schematic form in Figure 1.

PROFESSIONALS

PROFESSIONS

|

DIVISION OF LABOUR

|

SOCIAL LIFE

|

NEEDS, DESIRES, PREFERENCES, VALUES, INTERESTS, ETC.

Figure 1.

By saying that the existence of professions is based on general human needs and values we do not mean to imply that professional groups would or should officially organize themselves around the needs of society as a whole. The primary task of the associations of physicians, lawyers, soldiers, teachers, journalists, scientific researchers, business executives, social workers, police officers, civil engineers and others is to further the interests and ideals of their own numbers, and to maintain the autonomous status of the calling by controlling the selection, education and initiation of new members as well as by monitoring the rights, privileges and career development of the established membership. We do argue, however, that no professional group will last long unless it can be expected to perform a useful need based, value based or interest based function in society. Physicians and nurses are expected to promote health, lawyers are presumed to further justice, soldiers and police officers are supposed to provide individuals and nations with security, and other professionals are expected to have similar roles in social life.

It is our starting point, then, that the role of professions and professionals in society can be partly defined by the needs they are presumed to satisfy and by the interests they are supposed to promote. Another factor in the definition of professional groups is related to the actions performed by the individual members of these groups in the line of duty. The potential consequences and possible results of the actions of professionals are presented schematically in Figure 2.

Professional actions are, of course, expressly intended to meet human needs, to fulfil desires, to satisfy preferences, and to promote the values and interests of individuals and groups. These actions can, however, turn out to be harmful, offensive or costly to the clientele of the professionals in question, or to society at large. Both physical and psychological harm can be inflicted either on purpose or by mistake. Health care workers, for instance, often cause temporary or even permanent physical damage to their clients by cutting them with knives, exposing them to radiation and sticking needles into them. The prima facie harm is in the majority of these cases counterbalanced by the good effects of the treatment. But health care professionals can also make mistakes, and when they do, they can frequently inflict unnecessary harm on the patients.

The remarks concerning foreseen and unforeseen harm can be extended to cases where professional actions are offensive or involve high cost. Police officers may be forced to offend people's sensibilities when they investigate crimes which are regarded as taboos in the surrounding community. Similarly, there are cases in which civil engineers cannot recommend inexpensive solutions without endangering the objectives set by their clients. However, offence can also be caused unnecessarily by inexpert behaviour, and superfluous expenses can mount up through miscalculation, fraud, or professional over-zealousness.

PUBLIC DISAPPROVAL

LEGAL CONDEMNATION

UNFAVOURABLE MORAL
JUDGEMENTS
|

Harm   Rights

Offence   Autonomy

Expenses   Justice

|
Professional actions
|
PROFESSIONALS

PROFESSIONS

Figure 2.

In a purely consequentialist analysis, the actions of professionals can be assessed by comparing the satisfaction of needs and preferences to the harm, offence and expenses caused by those actions. According to deontological moral ideals, however, the ethical issues concerning professional conduct cannot be exhausted by mere calculations of utility. Professional actions can, so the proponents of deontological views argue, violate the rights of individuals and undermine the principles of autonomy and justice, quite apart from the physical harm and psychological offence inflicted on individuals or groups. It is possible, for instance, that molecular biologists violate the rights of future individuals by tampering with their genetic makeup.[2] It is also possible that health care professionals illegitimately invade the autonomy of their patients,[3] and that business executives act unjustly when they maximise the profits of their own corporations at the expense of the rest of society.

Actions which are potentially harmful and arguably immoral have, as a rule, met with public disapproval, legal condemnation, and the unfavourable judgements of moral philosophers. Harmful and offensive actions cannot be condoned unless their beneficial consequences can be shown to exceed considerably their undesired side effects. Violations of rights and autonomy, as well as deviations from justice, in their turn, have often been condemned regardless of the consequences. These points seem to imply that the majority of professional actions ought to be rejected as immoral.

The actions of professionals cannot, however, be directly compared to other harmful and offensive activities. Professional actions, unlike the acts of the person in the street, are regulated by professional codes, which should, ideally speaking, define the obligations and privileges of the agents in question. The role of professional codes is described schematically in Figure 3.

In general terms, the function of professional codes is to justify legitimate professional actions by pointing out their relationship with the needs, desires, preferences, values and interests they are supposed to serve, and by defining and rejecting those professional actions which are overly harmful or otherwise immoral. Well defined ethical codes form, figuratively speaking, a protective shield under which competent professionals can serve society without fear of public disapproval or legal condemnation despite the potential immorality of their actions.

A complete professional code enumerates both the obligations and the privileges of the vocation or association they are attached to. The positive rights and duties of the professional group (which have been placed inside the 'protective shield' of ethical codes in Figure 3) are directly or indirectly related to the satisfaction of the needs which ought to be promoted by the members of the group. The duties involved are positive and direct, and they have been explicitly stated in many existing codes of ethics.[4] Professionals of all descriptions have a firm obligation to satisfy the needs, to promote the interests and to respect the values of their clientele, as the fulfilment of this duty constitutes the basis of their privileged position in society. Members of vocational groups who are unable to provide the general public with useful services cannot be regarded as professionals in the full sense of the word. A guild of tinkers or an association of village blacksmiths would not find a proper place in modern urban communities.

The privileges of a profession include, most importantly, the right to perform the duties specified by the group's code of ethics. Physicians cannot protect people's lives if they are not, as a rule, allowed to submit their patients to the procedures required by state of the art medicine. Soldiers cannot protect nations if they are not permitted to kill and maim enemy soldiers, and police officers cannot perform their duties if they are not licensed to use force at least in certain specified circumstances. It may be the case, of course, that people do not want protection at the expense of the lives and liberty of foreign soldiers or domestic lawbreakers. But if they do, they should grant their protectors the privilege to employ the methods which they professionally deem necessary.

Positive professional rights and duties intersect in the domain of education and training. All those who want to become members of a given professional group must learn the skills required in the profession's work, and the established membership have a duty to keep step with the developments in their chosen field. These obligations can, however, also be seen from an entirely different angle. Many professional groups state that it is their rightful privilege to recruit, educate and initiate their own members, and some of these groups argue that society as a whole is responsible for providing the resources for the enforcement of the privilege. The duty of professionals to serve society should, so the argument goes, be reciprocated by the society's obligation to finance their education.

The negative rights and duties of a professional group (which have been placed outside the cover of professional codes in Figure 3) are centred on the obligation of professionals to abstain from unnecessary immorality in their work. The actions and consequences which should be regarded as unduly harmful, offensive or otherwise immoral are in many cases defined, either directly or indirectly, by the existing ethical codes. In the Hippocratic Oath, for instance, physicians directly promise not to 'give a deadly drug to anybody if asked for it', not to 'give a woman an abortive remedy', and not to 'use the knife, not even on sufferers from stone' (Beauchamp and Childress, 1983, p. 330). In the Physician's Oath of The World Medical Association Declaration of Geneva, on the other hand, the first two prohibitions are indirectly stated in a clause where the members of the profession pledge to 'maintain the utmost respect of human life from the time of conception' (Beauchamp and Childress, 1983, p. 331). The professional's duties to abstain from causing harm are, in fact, universal obligations which apply equally to all moral agents. But it is often necessary to embody them in ethical codes lest they be blurred by the existence of professional privileges and immunities.

140

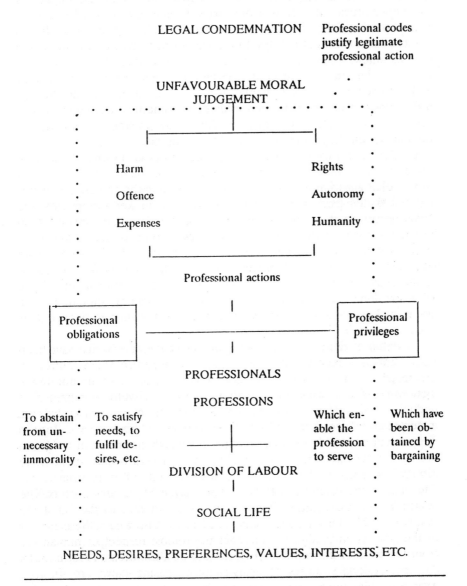

PUBLIC DISAPPROVAL

LEGAL CONDEMNATION　　Professional codes
justify legitimate
professional action

UNFAVOURABLE MORAL
JUDGEMENT

Harm　　　　　　Rights

Offence　　　　　Autonomy

Expenses　　　　Humanity

Professional actions

Professional
obligations　　　　　　　　　　　　　　Professional
privileges

PROFESSIONALS

PROFESSIONS

To abstain　To satisfy　　　　　Which en-　Which have
from un-　needs, to　　　　　　able the　been ob-
necessary　fulfil de-　　　　　profession　tained by
immorality　sires, etc.　　　　to serve　bargaining

DIVISION OF LABOUR

SOCIAL LIFE

NEEDS, DESIRES, PREFERENCES, VALUES, INTERESTS, ETC.

Figure 3.

141

The negative rights of professions and professionals are based on prevailing traditions and on contracts with the rest of society rather than on rational arguments or moral principles.[5] This is why these privileges can often be reasonably challenged in critical analyses. Consider the fact that police officers do not normally give a ticket to their fellow officers for minor traffic violations.[6] Should professional courtesies like this be regarded as legitimate examples of collegial solidarity or should they be seen as unlawful instances of official corruption? The answer depends on the effect that the collegial courtesies in question have on the profession's ability to serve the general public. It can be argued, of course, that the unity of law enforcement officers makes it considerably easier for them to serve and to protect other people. But it can also be argued that the double standards applied in giving tickets confuse their priorities in the line of duty, and eventually decrease their impartial willingness to serve others.

The contractual privileges of professionals include the economic and social benefits that they are granted in exchange for services to their community. Seen from the viewpoint of professional ethics, these privileges are justified only insofar as they enable the members of the profession to benefit their clientele. There are, to be sure, other arguments which state that individuals and groups are entitled to all the advantages that they can achieve in the free market. But since the supply of professional services is in many cases monopolized by trade unions and vocational associations, these arguments should be used cautiously in the context of professional privileges.

As stated at the outset of this paper, the existence of professions and professionals is based on human needs, desires, preferences, values and interests. This formulation does not explicitly recognize any differences between, say, the transient recreational desires of well to do minorities and the basic needs of the homeless or the starving. As regards the natural emergence of professions and professionals, this obvious difference between transient desires and basic needs is unimportant. But when it comes to the justification of professional life, the situation changes drastically. It is one thing to argue that the training of physicians to cure life-threatening diseases ought to be publicly funded, and quite another matter to claim that the education of professional concert pianists should be subsidized. There are, of course, difficulties which stem from the fact that a professional training often qualifies professionals to perform several tasks. Specialists in plastic surgery can devote their lives to restoring the features of accident victims, or they can dedicate themselves to becoming rich and famous by moulding the faces and bodies of actors and politicians. But the basic principle concerning , the legitimacy of professional rights is clear. Professions which serve the basic needs of individuals are entitled to more extensive privileges and benefits than occupations which are designed to satisfy less basic desires and preferences.[7]

Since human interests, preferences, values and desires are subject to alterations, and since the development of professional practices and skills frequently enables professionals to meet an expanding sphere of needs, justifiable ethical codes must be open to change. The Hippocratic Oath does not offer proper ethical guidelines to present day physicians, and the code of nurses which was valid in Florence Nightingale's time would presumably fail to define and to direct the work of today's nursing professionals. Groups who choose to ignore the changes which occur in society in general or within their own group often face considerable public pressures, and may eventually become the target of extensive legal regulation.

Notes

1. Our thanks are due to Mark Shackleton, Lecturer in English, University of Helsinki, for revising the language of the paper.
2. See, e.g., Häyry, M. (1993), 'Categorical objections to genetic engineering - a critique', in Dyson, A. and Harris, J. (eds.) (1993), *Biotechnology and Ethics*, Routledge, London and New York.
3. On autonomy and health care, see, e.g. Häyry, H. (1991), *The Limits of Medical Paternalism* , Routledge, London and New York.
4. See, for instance, the code of physicians and nurses reprinted in Beauchamp, T.L. and Childress, J.F. (eds.)(1983), *Principles of Biomedical Ethics*, Second edition, Oxford University Press, New York and Oxford, Appendix 2.
5. Many rights which are now regarded as traditional or conventional have, however, been obtained by bargaining in the past. Furthermore, even privileges which have never been explicitly the subject of bargaining can in the majority of cases be seen as results of implicit trade-offs.
6. See, e.g., Kleinig, J. with Yurong Zhang (1993), *Professional Law Enforcement Codes: A Documentary Collection*, Greenwood Press, Westport, Connecticut, pp. 20-21.
7. Our thanks are due to those fellow participants of the Society for Applied Philosophy 1993 Annual Conference who drew our attention to these points during the discussion period.

References

Beauchamp, T.L., and Childress, J.F. (eds) (1983), *Principles of Biomedical Ethics*, Second edition, Oxford University Press, New York and Oxford.

11 Professional behaviour and the organisation

Christine Henry

Within current organizational change whilst the value of care is 'preached', another, competition, may be practised (Henry et al., 1992). To behave in a professional way means to practise within a moral frame of reference. Any organization will set goals and norms through its management structure, processes, style, policy and procedures which may or may not encourage moral or professional behaviour. Members of the organization's community, including leaders of that organization, are subjected to the structure and the processes within and to the pressure and demands from without. External ideological, political and economic factors impose their own influences on personal, professional and organizational integrity.

Accountability is a concept central to practising what is preached. Ideally professional accountability is central to the setting of standards and norms and persons within the organization are responsible for planning and managing quality and delivery of the service, both individually and collectively. From a professional perspective there is personal and collective accountability for establishing and maintaining the standards of practice. There ought to be shared professional and organizational values but how are we able to identify these?

According to Wilcox and Ebbs (1992) the word 'professional' has an historical origin within a religious community. This directly relates to being a member of a particular community and to the making of a commitment of a particular kind. Both religious communities and professionals may share similar values. Furthermore, the general public and the professionals themselves may generally perceive the public or private organization as a valued, and necessarily caring community.

Central to ethical practice and the idea of a caring community is an understanding of important moral principles and values. It is essential for both moral integrity and credibility for assessing good practice that shared principles and values are implicit within professional codes of behaviour or a general organizational code or mission statement, if there is a serious attempt to practise what we preach. Principles are guidelines for human conduct. They have a broad universal application and are central to the ways in which we behave towards each other. For example the principle of respect for persons will always have important implications for caring/professional communities (people organizations) including management, and for the professions collectively. 'Most western, principle-based ethical systems have long tended to consider respect for persons a central and indispensable normative principle in moral reasoning' (Keyserlingk, 1993).

Respect for persons is the central principle of professional practice. Henry and Pashley (1990) accept the view that the term 'person' is a value laden term like the moral term 'good'. If the term person is used like a moral term then it follows that respect for persons is an important moral principle inherent in professional practice, upholding the values inherent in management practice. Furthermore respect for persons is a central principle that relates to other principles such as autonomy, nonmaleficence, beneficence, equity and justice. Respect and value not only involve other regarding aspects and principles of care but emphasize that we give person status to others. With personhood goes rights, responsibilities, and personal autonomy. If respect for persons is not both the focus and guiding principle to both the professional codes and the organizational goals, than it follows that the individual will be disadvantaged. We are all aware from social history of the consequences for a race of people who had their person status taken from them (Germany, World War II). When individuals are not treated as persons or valued as individuals, unethical practices occur. From one perspective, for example, within the organization, an individual may be perceived only as a 'cost unit'. This example may be over-simplified, but serves to remind us of what can and does happen if principles are not in any sense used as the guideline and where lip service is paid to a charter, a mission statement or code of professional conduct.

According to Henry et al. (1992) values are much more subjective than principles and are not necessarily moral. Some organizational values may conflict with professional or personal values (when competition is the only organizational value). Values have a personal interpretation, they can violate or support principles. Wilcox and Ebbs (1992) remark that when institutions look towards a form of self-assessment they are required to assess progress through a commonly held bench mark. This bench mark is articulated through the mission or value system. However, in relation to substantiating a professionally ethical driven system, the values that are

146

shared and involve practising what we preach in both professional and organizational terms, must support moral principles.

Charters, mission statements and codes

Professional standards and codes are usually perceived as guidelines to generally accepted norms. According to Bellah et al. (1985) charters and codes are often necessary when a culture is undergoing change and where a lack of consensus of values may become evident.

Charters are statements that involve a summary of good practice and the identification of standards. A charter will reach a wider audience and is broadly interprofessional in essence. A charter will reaffirm fundamental principles and values. However, difficulties arise both in their construction and implementation, if they are imposed upon an organization from the top down without a sense of ownership by the members of that organization's community. Identifying standards and ways to improve those standards ought to be encouraged through research based value audits that capture the values, principles and perceptions of all the stakeholders within and across the organizations. The same process may be applied to mission statements. Whilst mission statements are broad statements of intent they form the first phase in a process that attempts to enhance practising what we preach. However, the most obvious criticism arises where the mission statement is totally at odds with the behaviour of the members of the organization.

Codes are specific to particular professional groups. Like charters, codes set guidelines for standards and must have identified principles that underpin practice. A code of professional conduct as a guideline for good practice may still not be widely known or its purpose appreciated by individuals within a specific profession. According to Heywood Jones (1990) knowing the code gives personal advantage and benefit to the profession as a whole. It is the responsibility of every professional to conform to their code and those who violate it may and do find themselves the subject of peer investigation. This professional self-scrutiny is based upon the principle of respect for and protection of the public. Likewise the same may be applied to an organization mission statement and any organization code. A code extends the perimeters of a charter by giving directives to the professional (including managers) and is concerned with professional regulation and the individual's professional conduct. Codes therefore must be continually evaluated and monitored and the guidelines explicitly stated so that directives may be taken to guide practice. Mission statements, charters and codes may well form at least part of the process of practising what we preach. However, it seems highly

147

relevant and perhaps essential to find ways in which existing charters, mission statements and codes can be evaluated, monitored or modified, and credible processes in which new codes and charters can be developed. There is some requirement to identify organizational values in order to develop realistic mission statements, charters or codes that will enhance good practice and in turn raise the ethical profile of the professionals and the organization. In some cases an organization may only require a mission statement rather than a code of practice. A charter may be more functional, working across professionals and organizations and could be national or international. However, perhaps a major point to consider is when should a charter be developed, prior to or after missions and codes? If mission statements and codes were constructed through in-house research, this information could feed into national research that would identify broad principles and values in order to substantiate the development of a realistic charter that had credibility. A major ethical concern lies with formulating a charter, a mission statement or a code that is not owned by the members of the community. It may be perceived as imposed upon the members arriving out of thin air. The members either are unsure how it has been constructed or have not participated in its development. One of the problems that arise and may cause conflict is a mismatch between organizational and professional values. In some cases a sense of helplessness arises if the mission statement, charter or code is unrealistic and cannot be put into practice. Perhaps it is through mission statements, charters and organisational codes that professional managers can share similar goals and directives with the specific professions.

An ethical management tool — the Ethics and Values Audit (EVA)

Do we practise what we preach? It is from this question that an Ethics and Values Audit (abbreviated to EVA) evolved. The EVA is a management tool that facilitated an examination and identification of shared principles and values underpinning mission statements, charters and codes. Furthermore, it can be seen as the first stage in a process for managing change. Wilson (1993) remarks that in years to come when many more organizations may be conducting ethical audits the EVA will be seen as the first serious attempt to quantify the profound effects ethics and values have on both organizational behaviour and performance.

The EVA may be applied to all members within the organization including those who manage. It examines something fundamental to an organization's stability, i.e. the facilitation in both staff and clients of awareness of their own moral lives and those of the organization's culture. Wilcox and Ebbs (1992) state that morality not only concerns individual and social welfare but is very much a part of the institutional landscape. An EVA is the beginning of an ongoing process of self-evaluation.

The EVA questions the notion of whether a highly moral corporate culture exists within any organization and how any organization is able to uphold and achieve its mission when it is faced with social, economic and political pressures. Furthermore, it addresses some of the problems that arise when market forces are imposed upon the public sector services and values appear to conflict. It is clearly identified that the impetus for an EVA emerged from a recognition of: 'the perception of a double standard, the impact of change, and the sensitivity to values and moral life that characterise these times' (Henry et al., 1992, p. 2).

Henry et al. (1992) remark that the process of identifying and exploring values and principles involves research, analysis and debate of the outcomes in order to discover ways in which to enhance ethical practice within an organization. Organizations attempt to enhance their professional standing by presenting a high ethical profile and by adhering to their mission, charters and codes of practice. This is crucial both for the organizations and their professional members particularly in times of change. What we do as well as what we say provides the application of implementing values into practice.

The EVA was based upon four premises involving the identification of values underpinning an organization's mission statement, how the values are shared and practised, the staff and clients' perceptions of values and how the organization would better fulfil its responsibilities to the society it serves. The objectives included producing a profile of shared values supporting them by ethical principles, an examination of organizational policy, recommending ways to enhance policy and practices and an understanding of ethical issues and ways to resolve problems.

The project was research based and involved capturing the day to day concerns of the organization. The main ethical principle is respect for and dignity of persons as well as recognition of the needs of the organization. The outcome of the EVA resulted in a three part comprehensive report.

Part one examines the purpose of the project, identifying the aims and presenting the results of the research based audit through ten themes highly relevant to the specific organization. These themes identified issues regarding informal networks, mutual respect and trust, peer group integrity, honesty and openness, interpersonal relationships, organizational decision making processes, styles of management, management practice, use and abuse of power and the provision of resources. Whilst these themes are of specific value to the individual organization the development of a profile may be transferable to others. Wilson (1993) remarks that the process of an ethics audit maps out how values are shared between the goals and objectives of an organization and codes and

149

the individual's own values and beliefs.

An organisation is structurally an entity in itself. Certain values can be imposed upon it in terms of its public image and explicitly stated goals and objectives. However, the organisation is also a reflection of the beliefs and values of the individuals within it. The two sets of value systems may not always be the same (Henry et al., 1992, p. 8).

Not only is it important to identify the shared values but also those values that are not the same. Whilst the quality of the shared values, goals and activities are reflected in and through the working relationships within the organization the differently held values if viewed as conflicting will also be reflected through both achieved and unachieved goals of the organization. The EVA report at the beginning of Part one states that if the organization's attitude does not match how staff see themselves and their role cooperation will eventually be withdrawn. Furthermore, if psychological needs are ignored in a context of poor communication, endless conflicts arise. The EVA was in one sense a preventive strategy in that after examining the organizational culture, finding out both positive and negative aspects, it seemed realistic to develop an action plan or a list of recommendations that perhaps would address some of the issues of concern. A cluster of values derived from the interviews and values grid was identified which the organization could practice in order to encourage a more stable psychological contract with its members. Whilst the formal contract relates to salary conditions and employee terms of reference, there is a psychological contract that is implicit. The psychological contract involves expectations, attitudes, self-esteem, self-worth, loyalty and respect which influence the individual's willingness to work and make personal sacrifices for the organization. The values identified included openness, good communication, collaboration, responsibility, respect, awareness, being valued, trust, integrity, accountability and professionalism. One respondent stated:

One qualitative aspect is that we have got [ethics]... on the agenda and that to me is a positive aspect of the institution which has accepted its responsibilities (Henry et al., 1992, p. 9).

The analysis of the data allowed for a credible list of recommendations which included issues related to styles of leadership and management, ways of improving the organizational culture, a review of the mission statement and the development of an organizational code of practice which should be consistent with the mission statement, policy statements and the organization's charter for management initiative. Further recommendations involved ways to improve communication, development of a learning community, ways to improve the environment and an ethics and values audit for students/clients. The recommendations were open for debate and seminars were arranged encouraging feedback from staff.

> The Recommendations are not (nor could be) explicitly ethical or moral. They represent an attempt to encourage a University management style and culture in which recognition of and respect for all members of its community is the paramount value and where a climate of genuine trust, participation in decision making and collaboration is fostered. The assumption then is good and fair ethical practice will naturally evolve and become the norm...(Henry et al., 1992, p. 32)..

Part two of the EVA report introduces ways in which an ethics audit may be carried out. Six methods of data collection were used. These included a questionnaire, an open ended interview technique, a values identification grid, case studies through an ethics hot-line, analysis of policies and a curriculum analysis. The sample of respondents for the research project was selected on a non-experimental basis. The research team made a conscious decision to utilize several methods for collecting data, in order to validate and encourage credibility for the exploratory research project. The principles of confidentiality and anonymity were of paramount importance in order to protect those respondents who participated in the project. The audit research team received 395 completed questionnaires, carried out 56 individual interviews, received 102 completed values grids and 50 case studies. A total of 603 members of staff participated in the ethics audit out of a total of 1200. Wilson (1993) states that an audit's methods involve moving from mission statements and codes through to examining the way in which an organization supports and nurtures its values. It therefore may be relevant to briefly give a summary of the organization's policy analysis. It seemed impossible to complete a policy analysis of all the organizational policy documents simply because of the time restriction in carrying out the audit, therefore selective policies were chosen that seemed highly relevant and important for the nurturing of the organization's values. It was stated at the outset that staff ought to familiarize themselves with the organizational policies and that a process of continual review ought to occur in order to monitor changes. The organization did have a specific policy on ethics and the development of an ethics committee. It was advised that the ethics policy be revised to include a more active role of the ethics committee addressing issues of both professional behaviour and research practice. The findings from both the interview and case study data indicated that an organizational code of professional practice ought to be constructed which would support both research and management practice. One respondent clearly stated:

> I think it is paramount that we research and we research properly, but we must research ethically (Henry et al. 1992, p. 18).

The organization had an equal opportunities policy which involved removing unfair discriminatory practices. Whilst the organization had developed a good framework for recognizing the centrality and importance of equal opportunities the policy analysis not only supported the idea for continuous review but that the equal opportunities committee should be more active with specific roles identified. It was necessary to develop further a coherent framework in which to operationalize policy. The findings from the data reflected a need to improve the 'psychological feel' or climate of the organization to ensure fair and just treatment. Most case study data related to the dissatisfaction with how individuals were treated.

Part three focuses upon major principles that are essential to applied ethical theory. The principles of autonomy, nonmaleficence, beneficence and justice are debated and shown to be closely related to the principle of respect for persons. There is a discussion on defining ethics and values. This substantiates the process as a values audit firmly locked into an applied ethical system for practice. Part three attempts to formulate the theoretical framework that underpins the audit.

> Values encompass not only morality but political, social, economic and aesthetic aspects of life (Henry et al., 1992, p. 109).

Values are central to a society's culture attitudes behaviour and involve individual personalities as well as groups.

> They flow from basic assumptions or world views, are the wellspring of the moral life and deeply influence ethical enquiry of that life (Henry et al., 1992, p. 109).

Whilst values embrace a diversity, in common sense everyday language the terms 'values' and 'morals' are used to mean the same. The EVA takes the position that moral values refer to modes of behaviour and held or shared values. Valuing actually captures the idea of both knowing and doing. The EVA was and is concerned with how we think about and act towards others and how features of the environment including other people's behaviour influence individual, professional and organizational thought and behaviour. It is hopefully self-evident that moral values and the process of valuing concern thought and action and the notion of self-reflection provides the impetus for ethical analysis and debate. Ethics by definition assesses the ways in which we behave and the values that we hold. The EVA project also was concerned with other instrumental values such as self-affirmation and competence. These values may not be directly seen as moral values but nevertheless are still within an ethical framework in that if they are influenced by poor communication or bad management strategies, levels of competence and aspects of self-affirmation will be affected. Enhancement of such instrumental values is essential for fulfilment of the organization's mission. Personal and organizational life guided by shared values and moral strategies will empower and affirm members of the organization's community. However, it is worth remembering that a balance is required in that:

> While it is a truism that the unexamined life is not worth living the life that is constantly under the microscope of ethical analysis in order to catch immorality, will not be worth living either (Henry et al., 1992, p. 110).

Whilst any organization will be influenced to some extent by external forces it is also driven by and shaped to some extent by internal ones (Tierney, 1988). The culture of an organization will be reflected through its achievements. Exploring the community, individual and group values gives not only a picture of an organization's culture but also a profile of what the potential development for that organization might be. Covey (1989) suggests that values are maps that emerge from experience and have a subjective interpretative reality, while principles are guidelines to human conduct with some enduring moral values. Principles are essential to theory and provide standards for behaviour.

Ethics as a discipline is seen as part of theoretical inquiry within the philosophical field but it is also part of every day common sense in that through interaction with others individuals make certain choices. Ethics offers ways of inquiry into behaviour and gives justification for actions based upon those choices. Professional ethics is within the field of normative ethics and concerns professional behaviour, judgement and choices. Within both public and private organizations members of the community will be mainly concerned with professional issues whether they are members of a specific profession or organizational network. Understanding through application of ethical theory may help resolve conflict. A moral dilemma occurs when an individual has to choose between two competing goods. For example one may act in the best interest of staff or clients and the organization but such action may mitigate against one's own best interest. The professional or manager may act in the best interest of the organization but may find herself in conflict with her own personal values.

Conflicting obligations to employees and clients may pull the organization in different directions. A synthesis of applying ethical theories may result in a common sense morality. However:

> Common sense is not always the most reliable guide for sound moral principles (Henry et al., 1992, p. 115).

Whilst it is very difficult to resolve moral dilemmas even through applying moral theory, identification of conflicting obligations in aspects of fairness, and respect for persons, are of paramount importance. Furthermore raising levels of ethical awareness and what constitutes good practice is essential for both the professional and the organization. Charters, mission statements and codes will not solve moral dilemmas but one of their functions involves raising levels of ethical awareness and hopefully encouraging ethical practice. Beyerstein (1993) remarks that codes serve important functions and that moral dilemmas can often be resolved by recourse to moral theory.

> The stronger the ethos is in ethical values within the culture of an institution, the more distinctive the institution will appear (Henry et al., 1992, 123).

Conclusion

According to DeMarco and Fox (1986) everyone theorizes about values — it is not limited to discussions between moral philosophers. Often disciplines other than philosophy will use moral theories of one kind or another to justify their own activities and try to resolve the problems within their own professional field. Members of the organization's community including the mangers are not exempt from this form of activity. In fact it is essential in everyday management practice. Whilst an EVA is at least in part the beginning a process that can be applied to organizations in order to assess practices, it is also driven by an ethical approach underpinned by professional ethics. Professional ethics encompasses principles and values central to normative inquiry.

It is clear that ethical issues arise in areas of management and professional decision making and involve individuals at all levels within the organization. Any leader within an organization is constantly under pressure from social economic and ideological forces and more than ever organizations have a requirement to respond to these societal pressures. There is constant concern for fair resource allocation, identifying priorities and informed decision making which will have many varied influences directly affecting the members of the organization's community. Ethical practice ought to be shared through adhering to principles and values related to practice and must permeate through the organizational values and management ethos.

> We'll raze it there's no other choice
> We'll raze it and from foundation to roof
> We'll build a new and decent house
> In which we shall live like human beings
> (Talat Sait Halman, quoted in Henry et al., 1992, p. 38).

References

Bellah, A. et al. (1985), *Habits of the Heart: Individualism and Commitment to American Life*, Berkeley University Press.

Beyerstein, D. (1993), 'The Functions and Limitations of Professional Codes of Ethics', in Winkler, E.R. and Coombes, J.R. (eds), *Applied Ethics A Reader*, Blackwell, Oxford.

Covey, S. (1989), *The Seven Habits of Highly Effective People: Restoring the Character Ethic*, Simon and Schuster, New York

DeMarco, J.P., Fox, M. (1986), *New Directions in Ethics: The Challenge of Applied Ethics*, Routledge and Kegan Paul, London, pp. 1-20.

Henry C., Drew J., Anwar N, Campbell G., Benoit-Asselman D. (1992), *EVA Project: Ethics and Values Audit*, University of Central Lancashire, Preston, UK.

Henry, C., Pashley, G. (1990), *Health Ethics*, Quay Publishers, Lancaster.

Heywood Jones, I. (1990), *The Nurses Code*, Macmillan, London.

Keyserlingk, E.W. (1993), 'Ethics, Codes and Guidelines for Health Care and Research: Can Respect for Autonomy be a Multi-cultural Principle?' in Winkler, E.R. and Coombs, J.R. (eds), *Applied Ethics: A Reader*, Blackwell, Oxford.

Tierney, W.G. (1988), 'Organisational Culture in Higher Education: Defining the Essentials', *Journal of Higher Education*, vol. 59, no. 1, Ohio State University Press.

Wilcox, J.R., Ebbs, S.L. (1992), *The Leadership Compass: Values and Ethics in Higher Education*, George Washington University, Washington D.C.9.

Wilson, A. (1993), 'Translating Corporate Values into Business Behaviour *Business Ethics European Review*, vol. 2, pp. 103-105.